T0000563

Downstairs Church

DOWNSTAIRS CHURCH

FINDING HOPE IN THE GRIT OF ADDICTION AND TRAUMA RECOVERY

CAROLINE BEIDLER MSW

NASHVILLE

NEW YORK • LONDON • MELBOURNE • VANCOUVER

Downstairs Church
Finding Hope in the Grit of Addiction and Trauma Recovery

© 2023 Caroline Beidler, MSW

All rights reserved. No portion of this book may be reproduced, stored in a retrieval system, or transmitted in any form or by any means—electronic, mechanical, photocopy, recording, scanning, or other—except for brief quotations in critical reviews or articles, without the prior written permission of the publisher.

Published in New York, New York, by Morgan James Publishing. Morgan James is a trademark of Morgan James, LLC. www.MorganJamesPublishing.com

Proudly distributed by Ingram Publisher Services.

All scripture quotations, unless otherwise indicated, are taken from the *Holy Bible: New International Version, NIV.* Copyright © 2011 by Biblica

Morgan James BOGO™

A **FREE** ebook edition is available for you or a friend with the purchase of this print book.

CLEARLY SIGN YOUR NAME ABOVE

Instructions to claim your free ebook edition:
1. Visit MorganJamesBOGO.com
2. Sign your name CLEARLY in the space above
3. Complete the form and submit a photo of this entire page
4. You or your friend can download the ebook to your preferred device

ISBN 9781631959783 paperback
ISBN 9781631959790 ebook
Library of Congress Control Number: 2022938851

Cover Design by:
Rachel Lopez
www.r2cdesign.com

Interior Design by:
Christopher Kirk
www.GFSstudio.com

Morgan James is a proud partner of Habitat for Humanity Peninsula and Greater Williamsburg. Partners in building since 2006.

Get involved today! Visit MorganJamesPublishing.com/giving-back

For Alex, Kayla and Amanda

TABLE OF CONTENTS

Introduction: Binding Wounds xi

Part 1: Bright Ashes 1
Chapter 1: The Dusty Road 3
Chapter 2: Broken, Beautiful 9
Chapter 3: Dumpster Fires and Deserts 19
Chapter 4: If You Know the Ship is Going Down 27
Chapter 5: Thorns that Testify 35
Chapter 6: One is Never Enough 43
Chapter 7: Stings on its Way Down 51
Chapter 8: Beauty from the Ash Heap 57

Part 2: Up from the Basement 69
Chapter 9: Testing the Waters 71
Chapter 10: No Laser Light Shows, Please 79
Chapter 11: Sweet Balm for a Broken Soul 89
Chapter 12: Flutter by Butterflies 99
Chapter 13: Broken, Unbroken Promises 109
Chapter 14: Me, Too 119

Chapter 15: Shaking from My Heart to My Feet 125

Chapter 16: Grass-Stained Jesus Groupies 135

Chapter 17: Show Me Brittle 141

Part 3: Beauty Upstairs 151

Chapter 18: Get Real (for Real) 153

Chapter 19: Shine a Light 159

Chapter 20: Conscious Contact 165

Chapter 21: Are We There Yet? 177

Chapter 22: There Is Power 185

Chapter 23: The Heart of the Matter 197

Conclusion: Now What? Do Something 207

Appendix A: Study Guide for Small Groups
        or Just Your Lovely Self 209

Appendix B: Additional Resources 217

Acknowledgments 219

About the Author 221

Endnotes 223

*From the downstairs church I learned
radical honesty and radical dependence.
We can't make it on our own.*

— Philip Yancey

Introduction:
BINDING WOUNDS

The mirror in the hallway of my grandfather's small duplex had tiny flecks of gold around its periphery, somehow stuck in the glass. I stood staring, my brows bending as I dissected each of my physical characteristics, one by one, with disgust. How I loathed everything about my eleven-year-old appearance. Nothing made me feel even an ounce of gentleness towards myself—not my poof of bangs that were the perfect elevation or my vanilla skin that smelled like Dove soap.

What brought the most disgust was a tiny, malformed ear lobe. I was born with a minor deformity or birth defect. My left ear lobe is about half the size of my right, more perfect lobe. *If only my ear was normal,* I thought to myself. *If only I could wear my hair up like the other girls. If only I wasn't so different. Ugly. Broken.* These thoughts fired back at me as I looked at myself with shame and disgust. A tiny thing like an ear lobe brought me to such a place of self-hatred and insecurity. I remember feeling so small and lost and confused.

I used to dream of becoming eighteen when I would be old enough to have surgery to fix the ear. They could take skin from another part of my body like my butt (said the doctor) and remold a new lobe to match the other one. Eighteen came and went, then twenty-eight and now thirty-eight. The last thing I want now is a "rear-ear" and I wear my hair up all the time, both ear lobes freely exposed to the elements. Looking back on this moment now, I recognize that it was about so much more than that tiny piece of missing skin. There were so many other factors that contributed to my feelings of worthlessness and brokenness and otherness as a child and then later as a teen and young adult.

In one of Philip Yancey's best-selling books, *What's So Amazing About Grace*, he talks about the two churches he encountered when he lived in Chicago: the church upstairs and the church downstairs. The upstairs church was where the traditional congregation met in their Sunday best, with polite nods and an out-of-pitch choir. There might be stained glass or newly installed strobe lights. There might be extending of the peace and collection plates or emotional altar calls and fiery baptisms. There might be friendliness and niceties and "I'm praying for you" and sometimes "Welcome."

The church downstairs that Yancey learned about was a 12-step fellowship where people struggling with alcoholism and addiction met. The room was dark and reminded him of a small cafeteria with retired, stained office chairs. The air smelled like cheap coffee and cigarettes. Yancey went with a friend several times to the room downstairs where chairs were arranged in an open circle. No option but to look one another in the eyes. What surprised Yancey most was the radical honesty.

He reflects: "One day I asked my friend Bob if he'd ever thought about visiting the upstairs church some Sunday. A look of alarm crossed his face. "Oh, I'd never go there!" he said. "Those people have their lives together. They dress so well, they have jobs, they show up on time. We're just a bunch of alcoholics. We smoke cigarettes, drink coffee, and try to keep each other from falling apart."

How sad that Bob saw church as a place for people who have everything together. Somehow, we Christians can give off those vibes, when actually we gather in church because we know we've failed, and we need God's grace and forgiveness. Like the downstairs church, we need a Higher Power that only comes from God and from the supportive community around us. God can only work with us when we admit our need. We must have open hands.[1]

Today my husband and kids joke about my ear lobe and it is the best and most amazing thing. My husband calls it "Lisa Lobe." My four-year-old daughter and son (I have twins) laugh, tug on it, and call it "baby ear." To see their joy at my expense, to realize how much shame and pain I've shed like a crusty cicada shell, brings such lightness and grace to the reflection I see when I look in the mirror today, and the reflection I see looking back at me through my children's eyes.

Along my journey of faith, a faith that resembles more what it's like to run the Tough Mudder and not so much that infamous scene with Julie Andrews in *The Sound of Music*, I've learned the weight of what this Bible verse really means: God heals the brokenhearted and binds up their wounds.[2] Whether that wound manifests as addiction, sexual violence, a weird ear, or all three. I've also spent time in both the upstairs and the downstairs church and I've learned how much one can learn from another about these wounds and about this binding up.

My journey has been messy and downright painful. It has been countless mirrors and innumerable ear lobes staring back at me laughing: you are not worthy of love. You are too different. Dirty. Broken. You don't belong here.

But my journey has also been filled with a surprising grace and hope that teaches me how to open my hands as I hear God whispering with tenderness: "Be real."

Part 1:
BRIGHT ASHES

Chapter 1:
THE DUSTY ROAD

For God so loved the world that he gave his one and only Son,
that whoever believes in him shall not perish but have eternal life.
– John 3:16

For God so loved the world? Whoever believed this and did not wrestle in aching doubt had no idea what living in the world was really like; the gritty, dark, unforgiving place I knew. And what is more, He gave up his son? Let him hang dripping with sweat and blood and writhing in anguish? And this was supposed to make me sing *Hallelujah*? Even if I tried back then, the words stuck in the back of my throat. I wanted to, but I couldn't understand. Believing in that Jesus seemed so artificial, untrue, so beyond what I thought I was capable of.

What I needed was an encounter. A living, breathing surrender—a catapult into faith. An experience that wasn't cloaked in tradition or subjugation or false narratives or pastel messaging. I didn't need to be preached at from an irrelevant pulpit or condemned for my transgressions. I didn't need to be looked down on or made invisible by people who only appeared to be spotless on the outside.

I needed truth.

Compassion.

Mercy.

Grace.

And I found that in recovery.

"I'm quitting again," Tanya said with a sigh. I looked up and caught the unsure path her eyes made around the room. She looked scared but resolved. I wondered why she decided to give up smoking. Most of us were slow to do this, sticking to the arguably faulty opinion that drinking copious amounts of energy drinks and vaping bubble gum juice or smoking old school like Audrey Hepburn would keep us relevant and sober.

Tanya smelled like cigarettes and Starbucks and was slumped in the black pleather chair next to mine, twirling a cinnamon stick between two fingers. She had a messy updo (the unintentional kind), wore an oversized sweatshirt and shiny black leggings. The rest of the room was filled with twenty-somethings hiding behind our fluorescent balayage, lip piercings, geometric tattoos or our less stereotypical looks: polos and khakis or blue scrubs or button-ups with matching Coach clutches. Hardly anyone made eye contact, including me. We kept our eyes fixed on the worn, dirty carpeting in front of us. Not really indifferent, but looking the part.

We each took our turn as the invisible baton was passed to the next person in the lopsided circle that made up our group. We introduced ourselves by saying our name, our drug of choice, and how many days we had in recovery. Most of the group had been together for a while, though occasionally newcomers would walk in even more sheepishly than we still did, terrified about what it was going to be like to have to tell the most shameful parts of our life stories to a room full of strangers. It was interesting, though, that the more we came back and showed up week after week, the easier it was to be honest. And the way we introduced ourselves had a strange way of making me feel at home.

Later that evening, when the sharing circled back to Tanya, she went on to tell our group what she was facing and how terrified she was. It wasn't just about the cigarettes. In a few short months, she was going to prison for her sixth driving under the influence or DUI. And she just found out she was pregnant.

"I'm not sure how long I'll have with the baby, but…" and her voice fell into tears.

The room echoed silence as we let the gravity of what she said sink in. This wasn't a Netflix series like *Orange Is the New Black*, this was real life. And the tough reality? What she was saying could have easily been any of our stories. It could have been me.

It turned out that she only had twenty-four hours after she gave birth to be with her precious baby girl. After these short hours, she was shackled and taken back to the prison from the hospital. She will never forget the sound of her baby crying as she was escorted down the cavernous hall. The way the leather and metal chains dug into her wrists. The smell of sweat and antiseptic. The way all she wanted to do was scream as loud as her baby, scream to make the walls fall down around her so she could scoop her daughter up like a baby chick and fly away.

Tanya spent another nine months in prison waiting without her.

I looked around the room at the ragtag bunch of us that were gathered there like tiny hatchlings who had fallen out of the nest but somehow survived. We were scared, unsure. Some of us shook as we spoke or our faces turned pink with flushes of both embarrassment and relief as we let each other into the darkest and most hidden parts of ourselves.

Being brought to your knees by addiction is an excruciating, yet freeing thing. All of the hard facades developed over time, the "I'm ok—see, look at how together I am"—none of this stands on firm ground. When you hit your version of rock bottom and are stranded in the shadowy depths, the only place left to look is up. The sacred lives in vulnerability.

From time to time, the well-meaning relative or long-lost high school buddy or church lady (said affectionately) has asked me why I continue to identify as an alcoholic and addict in some recovery spaces after living over a decade in recovery.

"Don't you graduate from recovery?"

"You've held off this long, one wouldn't hurt. Would it?"

"How long do you have to do those meetings anyways?"

I always have the same answer: I need to remember. My addiction to alcohol and other drugs that started long before my fourteenth birthday, took me down some dark and winding paths—many that, most days, I'd like to forget. And it is precisely this journey I've traveled that leads me to call myself by certain names in certain places. But importantly, I've learned on this broken road that this is not the whole of who I am. My identity is more than alcoholic or addict or survivor—or, as I like to say in *all* spaces: a woman in addiction recovery. Who I am is more than what I have done, or how I have been undone.

It's taken a bit of time for the dust to settle. While it is a part of my story, it's not the only chapter. For me, identifying as an alcoholic and addict with my recovery family does help me to remember where I've come from. When I share in meetings, whether those are in-person nestled in the basement of a church or virtual with people from another country, there is an instant familiarity that is expressed when those words are uttered. It doesn't matter if I live in another zip code, time zone, or all the way across the globe. Those simple identifiers open up a shared space where we can say, regardless of the particulars: "Me, too."

Something mysterious and healing happens when we open ourselves up to the real.

Alcoholic and addict. These two simple words that carry so much hurt and heartache and struggle also carry an important humbling reminder that I am not that far from returning to those dark places: driving down highways not remembering how I got there; spending the last of my money on a small baggie worth of hurt; letting go of family relationships that I should have held close; sharing my bed with people who never deserved to be there. I've been neck-deep in the dumpster (literally and figuratively) and somehow, indeed miraculously, have made it out to the other side alive. The side where there is light and sunshine and hope.

This new place, the one on the other side of the hard times, is where I also identify as so many other things: mother, wife, sister, builder, wannabe comedian (ask my husband), writer, dessert baker and destroyer, hiker, novice meditator, shower singer, neighbor-lover, Christian—and woman in recovery. All of who I am and who I am becoming was born after some pretty intense struggle and out of the identity of "alcoholic and addict," but thankfully, I have not stayed confined to those labels. I have allowed all of myself to move and grow and breathe as my Higher Power, my God, designs. And importantly, I've learned through the love of broken people that my brokenness can be beautiful, too.

Years later after she shook us with her honest fear about giving birth in prison in that small circle, I asked Tanya what the toughest part was. She said:

"The worst part was the profound shame. I was terrified about what this was going to mean for my daughter. What is she going to think about herself, that she was born in prison? One attorney asked me about aborting the baby—suggesting this might be easier. Some people even assumed I got pregnant on purpose to get a lighter sentence. There was so much judgement."

I could hear her voice quiver and get softer as she spoke.

"I still struggle with talking about it publicly because of the guilt. People think a certain way about people like me."

Chapter 2:
BROKEN, BEAUTIFUL

She knew I could tell with one glance, one look, one simple instant.
It was her eyes. Despite the thick makeup, they were still dark-
rimmed., haunted, and sad. Most of all though, they were familiar.
The fact that we were in front of hundreds of strangers changed
nothing at all. I'd spent a summer with those same eyes—scared, lost,
confused—staring back at me. I would have known them anywhere.
– Sarah Dessen

The cutting cold of the night numbed my cheek as I lay against a pillow of snow. My head was heavy—I could not lift it—but my eyes still looked around from my quiet place on the ground. No one. Silence. Maybe the faraway hum of traffic. Maybe a street light casting a yellow shadow on the parked cars. Maybe the taste of acidic peppermint in my mouth. I was glad to be alone. The crowd had become too suffocating.

Someone's parents were gone for the weekend and so a bunch of us decided to have an older brother buy alcohol. The one who smoked Camels and drove a Camaro. Boys in puffy coats sat around a kitchen table and played cards and girls in white jeans and turtle necks stood around sipping wine coolers. A couple of the boys were like me (needed more) and got a bottle of booze all to ourselves and started drinking it like water. After an hour of chugging too much of the sharp, peppermint liquid that burned my throat as it went down, that familiar spinning and heat in my head started. No one ever teaches you how to drink responsibly. I felt flushed, dizzy, and needed somewhere to go. Anywhere that wasn't there. I needed a place where the walls and floor and everything would stop spinning.

It was cold out but it felt good. So soft. I sunk down into the whiteness as I dropped to my knees and hit the ground, then fell over slowly on to my side. No one knew I was out there and that was perfect, because I was still trying to keep up appearances. I was still a "fun drunk." Cool, hilarious, charismatic. My drinking (or what I wanted to show of it) was in control. *I* was in control—for a freshman in high school.

"A moment," I remember thinking. "I will lay here for just a moment."

I'm not sure how many moments I was outside. After some time (could have been minutes, could have been hours), he was kind enough to find me and bring me inside. My breath danced like smoke in the air. He held under my arm with his arm, guiding me through muffled laughter. He pulled me up the short stairwell to the bathroom. I was so grateful for the help. I started feeling a pit in my stomach churn and knew I needed to be there.

Then, he kindly waited while I held my head over the toilet, holding my hair back and stroking my head sweetly like my grandpa used to do when I was sick as a kid. Almost half a bottle of Blue 100 and now it was coming back up violently along with the little bit of dinner I ate earlier. After I was completely empty, utterly spent, and still swirling-nauseous, I stood up and grabbed onto the sink with both hands. I tried to look at my face in the mirror but my head fell heavy down. His face came in to focus and he was smiling behind me. He helped to turn on the water so I could get a couple drinks with my hand. My thirst was maddening. The cool felt so soothing on my lips, traveling down my throat and into the empty place the alcohol left. I was starting to feel just a little bit better. I turned towards the bathroom door to leave. But he reached around me and locked the door.

I could hear the laughter coming in from under the doorway and could see shadows and movement as the walls continued to spin around me. *I think there are people outside*, I remember thinking but not having the ability to speak. I wanted to say something but my voice froze. My eyes strained to find something to hold onto as he lowered me to the ground softly and climbed on top of me. My sight came in to focus for a moment and I caught notice of my hair moving back and forth across the cold bathroom floor.

Everything happened like it was happening to someone else.

The next morning, I stood in the kitchen listening to my parents tell a story about their dinner the night before. They went out with friends. Pizza. Someone's daughter was doing so well. Someone's son just left for bootcamp. My brother came in and out of the room, wearing his workout clothes, getting ready for a run. Sipping water. Making peanut butter toast. All I could think about was wondering how I could sneak into the woods for a cigarette. My usual trick of fastening a makeshift cigarette holder using a pipe cleaner or paper clip so my fingers wouldn't be stained by the smell all day—would this work today? Because I really needed this to work today.

The phone rang and my heart dropped down into my feet.

It was his friend.

"Hey," I muttered.

"Hey."

There was silence on the phone. I looked at my parents who were continuing to tell their story and my brother who was doing calf stretches by pushing up against the marble counter top.

"So, he wanted me to call you."

My heart pounded with a glimmer of hope.

Maybe he wanted to start going out with me, I thought. He was, after all, one of the popular sophomores. He had only the prettiest girlfriends, the ones with all the newest clothes who drove Grand AMs or red Cavaliers and whose parents let them wear eye liner and dye their hair blonde all seasons of the year and stay out until midnight during the week.

There was more silence until I muttered: "Yeah?"

"He just wanted to—."

All of a sudden, I felt like I was choking. My chest tightened up and I got light-headed. I saw flashes of the night before and all at once it was all too overwhelming. As I started to hang up the phone, he said:

"Don't call him."

"Oh—okay," I whispered and the receiver clicked into place.

I walked to the counter where my cereal bowl sat with the milk I had just poured in it.

"Who was that?" my dad asked.

"No one."

The cereal was soggy and floating in the milk. I put the spoon into the bowl and swirled it around once and walked over to the sink and poured it down. My brother left for his run; the door closed behind him. My parents kept telling their stories from the night before and I silently made my way down to my bedroom and closed the door.[3]

The first time I heard the phrase "me, too," I was sitting in an apartment that I had recently moved to in Madison, Wisconsin, and had just learned of yet another violent rape that occurred only a couple of miles from campus and the small house where I lived. This latest hashtag phenomenon was a way that women all over the globe connected with each other and shared their experience of sexual abuse and assault and harassment; what had been kept in darkness and surrounded by shame for lifetimes for many was now being released out into the open. What many (including me) did not know was that the concept of "me, too" had actually been coined almost a decade or so earlier by a woman named Tarana Burke, who is an advocate for women of color who have survived sexual violence. I was both encouraged and a bit taken back by the forwardness of it all and not quite sure how I felt (I am from the Midwest). Only later did I realize that this was uncomfortable for me because it made me look at my own experience.

After the news of this horrific assault reached my little home, I was terrified every day to come home in the dark, terrified to fall asleep or let Mo (my pup, the best therapist money couldn't buy) out in the small backyard behind it. I lived adjacent to a dingy restaurant parking lot that was usually mostly empty except for one creepy Cadillac. Something straight out of a 1990s horror movie. Deep within me I had a sinking feeling and one that I could not shake: *it's time to move.* It was like my brain was rapid firing warnings that I could not push aside. I wanted to run as fast as I could from that little house and from the news and from what was happening in the world.

I went to church on a Sunday not shortly after and showed up the way I usually did—walking warp speed, making a beeline for the coffee area. I probably smelled like a crematorium (I was still smoking cigs back then) as I tried not to make eye contact and find a seat near the back exit. Always have an exit strategy—paid for that advice from my therapist. I looked around and saw families and cool-looking twenty-somethings that made me feel like such a phony. I wanted to believe their message of a gracious God, I wanted to have mountaintop moments, but it was hard. I'll just say it. It's hard to break into something that from the outside looks so untarnished.

Sometimes women around my age smiled at me with closed lips or nodded, but they usually had a glittering ring and a baby on their hip—two things that reminded me how much my life hadn't quite turned out the way the movies say it should. Or if these nice, nodding women were single, they were usually surrounded by other "singles" (that's churchy for unmarried) with the latest trends in fashion and expensive purses. I often wondered: what would Jesus think about all these purses?

I looked different on the outside, not being able to afford the trends and not really caring so much anyways; and more importantly, I felt different on the inside. I was almost sure if they knew me, they wouldn't let me in to this place. Even though it used to be a strip mall or car dealership or, in the case of the latest church I was trying out, a downtown bar and music venue that morphed into a "relevant" and Gen Z-friendly church on Sundays.

That particular Sunday, the pastor with blonde spikey hair, Italian leather shoes and a cardigan for some reason (it was warm in there), preached something about something from the Bible as I tried to stay in my seat. I had had the experience in the past of panic attacks during a sermon because of having to sit too close to someone I didn't know. Or like this particular Sunday, I couldn't stop thinking about the violent attack that happened so close to where I lived. When the lights dimmed and the worship band walked on stage, I knew this was the perfect time to sneak out. I needed to breathe the air that wasn't in there.

The writer of Lamentations, argued to be Jeremiah, witnessed terrible suffering in his day: the Babylonian invasion and destruction of Jerusalem around 586 BC. Jeremiah recounts what it was like to walk through the desolation of what was once a vibrant city. He laments in such grief that you can almost hear it through the pages of scripture. He was also terrified, being hunted like a bird, persecuted and even thrown in a pit. The people of Jerusalem were living the effects of sin in the world, with Jeremiah experiencing the effects of this firsthand.

Jeremiah wept bitterly and cried out to God in response.

And God's reply: "Do not fear."[4]

Now don't get me wrong—I am not a Bible scholar or theologian. My daddy is not a preacher. I have never attended seminary (unless the free online classes from Dallas Theological Seminary count) and have only been to a Honda hatchback of Bible studies over the years (shout out to BSF![5]), but there is something mysteriously true and sacred about the words found in that big book that for most of my life sat on a dusty shelf untouched. And the many people in it, like Jeremiah or the Apostle Paul or Ruth or the woman caught in adultery, or even Jesus himself, often remind me of my own struggles and journey and strangely reflect back to me the longings and quandaries and breakable humanness of my own heart. I like the way Philip Yancey puts it: "I'm not a theologian or pastor, I'm a pilgrim."

The phrase "fear not" appears in the Bible 365 times, one time for each day of the year. How appropriate. It seems like God likes repetition and likes to tell his people not to fear when they are riddled with it and unsure of how anyone—including Him—is going to show up to make everything okay. I find this to be somewhat humorous when things are going well for me and a little more than annoying when they are not. Excruciating even. Though Jeremiah was tortured by what he saw around him—the pain and the people, including women and children, suffering— God told him not to be afraid. That somehow, in the end, it was all going to make sense and be okay.

Rick Warren, pastor of Saddleback Church in Lake Forest, California, says that "hurts and hang-ups can often cause us to think that God is out to get us, that all He wants to do is condemn us and punish us. But that simply isn't true."[6] Even though I knew that God was not some Marvel villain out to get me, this story of this latest attack on a woman in the city I loved drove me to despair and reminded me of what I had lived through, and made me question again what God thought He was doing anyways. Like Jeremiah, I looked at the city where I lived and I wept for that woman whose scars, visible and invisible, might take years to heal as mine did. I pictured her, with brown unwashed hospital hair and sunken eyes, laying in white sheets that smelled like bleach and turning her face away whenever a nurse came in to check her vitals or another officer had her go through the details of the attack. Again—and again and again. I pictured her living near the dingy restaurant, shaking when she heard a loud noise at night, afraid to open her door when she heard a knock that she wasn't expecting.

My new apartment—where I escaped to—was on the outskirts of town, in one of those new developments that have been built up where once only fields of farmland existed. As soon as I got five miles from the city's downtown it felt like I could finally breathe. There were trees and rich sunsets and neighbors right next door. The air smelled like cornfields, like in the small town where I grew up. The shiny faucets and clean white wood, the views of the fields and crisp air that hit my face on the boardwalk as I walked Mo—all of these things were pictures of my new life, my changed life. In actuality, I was not really safer than I was when I lived in that little house downtown, but something felt safer here. When I needed to leave a situation, I could.

Addiction recovery is about so much more than quitting alcohol and other drugs. For me it is a peeling back of many layers, like an onion—or to liven up the vegetable metaphor a bit, a cabbage. Before

I get ready to slice up some cabbage for one of my favorite stir fry dishes, I always pull the outer, dirty-brown leaves off first. Quitting alcohol and other drugs was like ripping those wilty leaves off first so I could get to the good stuff: the crisp, light-green leaves. But don't get me wrong—when I say "good stuff" I also mean hard stuff. Underneath the visible wilt was where it started to get interesting—and unbearably tough. My layers that I've had to work on over the years have been wrapped so tightly around each other they've been almost impossible to pull apart: layers of shame and brokenness and trauma. Things I've been afraid to even whisper about in the dark.

Recovery, for me, first started with the realization that I needed to change, that my life was unmanageable and wasn't working anymore. Then, after that it was a continual peeling back and learning and trusting that it was all going to be okay; I was going to heal, even when I was scared and even when what I saw or experienced, like Jeremiah, brought me to my knees with crushing grief. I was going to end up with a bowl of pretty chopped cabbage that would be excellent fried with a little sesame oil and a dash of ginger.

Though I felt uncomfortable and had to move away from what triggered me most, and it took everything in my power not to run to a thousand new places and a thousand safe spaces a thousand miles away, the day I heard "*me, too,*" a part of me also took a soft, quiet, healing breath. Every time I saw a new face, heard a new story—exhale. I've heard many women say the same: that the "me, too" movement has been a cathartic experience. Never had I heard these stories in church, but I looked online and followed the hashtags all across the country, some across the world. There were so many examples of hardship and pain endured, but most importantly, so much joy in the eyes and stories of redemption.

In searching for solidarity, I found a poem by a woman who had the courage to release her burden in the world through words. I did not yet have the courage to share my pieces of suffering or my story, but I could connect and share someone else's. A part of the poem signed only "A.V." reads:

I am afraid my bones will never regrow

I, without a body,

Cried into the night.

Me, too,

Came voices from everywhere.

"I am ashamed to wear this dark badge pinned into my chest"

Me too,

Sang the somber chorus,

Me, too…

Chapter 3:

DUMPSTER FIRES AND DESERTS

*I suppose one of the reasons we're all able to continue to exist for
our allotted span in this green and blue vale of tears is that there
is always, however remote it might seem, the possibility of change.*
— Gail Honeyman, Eleanor Oliphant

What's the first thing that comes to mind when you hear the word "addiction?" When was the last time you saw something about addiction on the nightly news or while you were scrolling on your phone? How was it portrayed?

This may be a startling fact: There are over 23 million Americans (and more than half of those women) who identify as being a person in recovery from addiction. That's a lot of people. Though in the world around us, addiction is rarely associated with something positive like recovery. If you are around my age (not telling) you might remember the stories upon stories about Lindsey Lohan and her wild red-maned shenanigans and less than glamorous bar-time photos or Charlie Sheen's interview (I needn't say more). Addiction in the news is focused on the cringe-worthy, shocking, and keeps us on the edges of our seats like the latest trending Netflix series or Britney Spears shaving her head in the early 2000s. Or Britney Spears today, for that matter.

In the news, we hear about the problem of substance use and dependence, ugly statistics about the opioid epidemic or about how drug dealers are destroying our cookie-cutter communities and stealing the futures of our brightest youth or from the offering plates. We are sometimes led to believe that addiction is only concentrated in poor urban centers, not in our own backyards, not in our church sanctuaries, not in our living rooms. We don't hear the real-life stories of success and hope: people in recovery starting families and raising children, graduating from college, buying homes, volunteering in their neighborhoods and faith communities, being great friends, spouses, siblings, daughters and sons. We don't hear about these everyday miracles and an important message is lost. We hear about Tanya's many failed attempts and convictions but we don't learn about her transformation and the incredible work she now does to help support those struggling in her community.

What about recovery? What about the millions of Americans and the hundreds of millions globally who have found a solution and now live transformed lives? What about the millions of resources available to help someone like me or like my family find the help that they need: medication-assisted treatments, community and faith-based supports, nonprofit organizations and small businesses, and countless other avenues that bring light into the darkness for those who struggle with addiction? What about the faith that God shakes through the "secular" circles of recovery spaces?

Marty Mann was one of the first women to be a member of Alcoholics Anonymous, and after entering recovery around 1940, she began telling her story. Because of her Christian faith and belief that

God called her to the task, she was tireless in her efforts to bring light to the realities of addiction and recovery, and was passionate about helping those "afflicted" with medical conditions who were, at that time, shunned by society. Because of her advocacy in the United States, the stigma surrounding alcoholism began to shift slightly and more people came to see it as a health issue (albeit with spiritual components) instead of a moral one.

We live in a very different world today than the one Marty Mann lived in, despite the prevalence of negative coverage about addiction in the media. You've likely seen on your newsfeed celebrities celebrating sobriety milestones or discussions about how billions of dollars of federal funding are going toward helping people struggling with opioid addiction (or maybe the algorithm doesn't allow it). Or perhaps, like me, you have even told your own story and brought it out of church basements and into a more visible sphere like social media to let others know that hope and change is possible.

Despite these positive strides forward, stigma sadly still exists—and sometimes especially in the faith community. Addiction is not viewed the same as other medical conditions, like cancer or diabetes, for instance. Can you imagine if your church decided not to let "those people" recovering from chemotherapy into your church after hours for fear they might steal the scarves from the kid's room? Or imagine not letting Chuck into the kitchen during the community meal preparation for fear he would sneak too many cookies and what would happen if he needed his insulin? Why, you are not a doctor.

What is stigma? I'll put on my teacher hat. The word "stigma" in Greek refers originally to a mark or brand on Greek slaves that separated them from free men or women. Slaves were branded so that they were clearly distinguished from those who were in upper classes. When they walked down the road, there was no mistaking. The dictionary definition now says that stigma is "a mark of disgrace or infamy." In a foundational work on the topic, *Stigma: Notes On the Management of Spoiled Identity*, Erving Goffman notes that it involves "an attribute that is deeply discrediting."[7] Those with substance use disorders are often seen as unpredictable or dangerous, and as a result, they suffer greater social rejection and isolation.[8] Stigma towards addiction is further perpetuated by attitudes that characterize the individual as at fault for their condition or immoral.[9]

Jesus was familiar with this concept. Those with conditions like leprosy were similarly shunned by society, as were women who were known to have committed sexual sins like adultery. Greeks, Gentiles, anyone who wasn't Jewish, gluttons, sinners—you know, Jesus' crew—all of these folks had scarlet letters of one kind or another that caused them to be outsiders, misfits, ragamuffins.

In John 8:2-11, the story of a woman caught in adultery is told. Jesus had been once again in the temple courts, a place where he frequently sat down to teach the people and the Pharisees and other teachers of the law. The people listened on and often tried to trap him in what he said. Today, the Pharisees and these teachers would most definitely be called "internet trolls" and probably hide behind their Twitter accounts or message boards to say some pretty revile and judgmental things. But I digress.

A woman was brought in who had been caught in adultery. These teachers shamed the woman by making her stand before the group. I imagine that she stood there with eyes looking towards the dirty ground, shifting her weight from one foot to the other, brushing away the mud and blood-caked strands of hair from her sweaty face.

The crowd looked towards Jesus and questioned:

Teacher, this woman was caught in the act of adultery. In the Law, Moses commanded us to stone such women. Now what do you say?

Of course, Jesus knew that they were trying to trap him so that they could finally catch him doing something "wrong," according to them. Of course, Jesus also evaded them by being super wise, as is his way (aka meta-woke). He bent down and began writing on the ground with his finger.

> *Let any one of you who is without sin be the first to throw a stone at her.*

And—mic drop.

Jesus very effectively, in one sentence, not only crashed their hopes of trapping him, but also humbled them all. How could they accuse this woman if they had also sinned—and likely many of them with the same sin of adultery that she was being accused?

Instead of addressing the crowd anymore, he turned away and continued to write on the ground. I like to imagine that he did a nonchalant hair toss before he snubbed them. Now, there is some speculation about what exactly Jesus was writing on the ground. No one knows for sure, but I like to envision that it was the lyrics to *Amazing Grace*, the lines that would later inspire the slave trader-transformed-abolitionist, John Newton.

Jesus also did not condemn the woman as they stood there while everyone left the temple courts one by one, like dogs who just stole the buttermilk biscuits off the counter, tails between their legs and ears back. He turned to her when everyone was gone—and this is important, this intimate moment between the two of them—and asks if anyone has condemned her (knowing full well the answer). After she answers no, he says:

> *Then neither do I condemn you [...] Go now and leave your life of sin.*

Jesus gave the woman a taste, perhaps for the first time, of grace. In *Traveling Mercies*, Anne Lamott says that grace is:

> [...] the force that infuses our lives and keeps letting us off the hook. It is unearned love—the clove that goes before, that greets us on the way. It's the help you receive when you have no bright ideas left, when you are empty and desperate and have discovered that your best thinking and most charming charm have failed you. Grace is the light or electricity or juice or breeze that takes you from that isolated place and puts you with others who are as startled and embarrassed and eventually grateful as you are to be there.[10]

Now, we don't hear any more from this woman in scripture, but we can assume that this encounter with a loving God changes her. We can assume that the grace "juice," as Lamott calls it, tastes pretty darn good like that super expensive ultra-organic grape juice at Whole Foods. We can assume that she does leave the life she had been living—whatever that looked like—and started again.

Stigma is very concerning for many reasons. It can prevent those with addiction issues from reaching out for help. It can also negatively impact the way they see themselves. It's like grace in reverse, a taking away of what God has promised us sinners.

In *What's So Amazing About Grace*, Philip Yancey talks about the origins of the Alcoholics Anonymous program. Founders Dr. Bob and Bill Wilson went to visit a lawyer who had been in and out of institutions and hospital wards and was restrained to a hospital bed in leather shackles. The worn-out and combative drunk had to listen to the white-haired teetotalers. Yancey writes that the visitors shared their recovery stories with the lawyer and how they discovered God, their higher power, through the process.

As soon as they mentioned their Higher Power, Bill D. (the lawyer) shook his head sadly. "No, no," he said. "It's too late for me. I still believe in God all right, but I know mighty well that He doesn't believe in me anymore."[11]

For many, struggling through addiction and other mental health challenges, grace feels far away, a chasm that can't be bridged. There is too much between a loving God and a dastardly child.

I'm sure this woman caught in adultery was not feeling too great about herself—whether or not she was actually guilty as the mob of people suggested (though it does seem like it as the text suggests she was caught). Either way—guilty or not, sexual immorality was highly stigmatized because women were forced to endure the public consequences and humiliation, whereas men were not.

Before I saw myself through God's eyes and truly felt grace, I was not willing to reach out for help or let that help really sink into my soul and change it. That sweet sound was so far away. Now, if the angry mob had condemned her instead of walking away one-by-one as they did, would the woman have had the courage to stand with Jesus and answer his call to repentance? If they forced her to wear her scarlet letter and shut her out (even unknowingly) from accessing the grace she so desperately needed, would she have turned towards a new road and new life at all?

Imagine if you turned on the evening news and heard a story of how love has greeted us on the way, before we deserved it, or a story about how we had met someone struggling in active addiction and said "yes, I see you and hear you and am here no matter what?" What if you saw in my teenage eyes the reason why I wanted to escape, why I spent so much time alone in the dark, and loved me anyway?[12]

Chapter 4:

IF YOU KNOW THE SHIP
IS GOING DOWN

The words were spoken by my entrails,
and by yesterday, not by me myself.
– Maria Duenas

In my early twenties, I changed my hair color almost once a month. It was as if the next box of smelly dye was going to bring me closer to being the "real me." Bleached or yellow-blonde, honey brunette, fire engine red, and then black. I can pretty much fit my early twenties in to each of these different color boxes, each of these different ways I tried to escape or become someone else. I rinsed the color out in the shower, toweled off my hair and looked in the mirror. The shade got a little brighter as my hair dried, but as I combed it out or pinned it back, the young woman staring back at me was still the same person. To my annoyance, I was always there.

Once when my hair was dyed black with matching (or not) purple-lined eyebrows, someone told me I looked like the WWF wrestler, China. I did not take this as a compliment back then (I totally would today). My idea of fun was smoking marijuana with my cat (seriously) and sipping on mocha lattes while writing pieces of stories that no one would ever read, and I would never read sober. The men I dated liked to do the same things I did, which revolved around smoking or drinking or both; and honestly, most of them were no fun to be around sober. By then, the panic attacks were almost daily, and the looming visceral sense that I was going to die at any moment was always two steps behind me. I did not know it at the time, but I was experiencing severe anxiety and depression because of the things that happened to me and some of the things I did. I'd later learn that there is a name for what I was experiencing.

For months, I painted on one canvas in oils every night when I got home from work. I'd sit at my small white kitchen table for one and pack Blue Crystal cannabis into a swirled red and yellow glass pipe and inhale deeply. Important to note in this little story is that I didn't consider myself an artist at all. But I didn't have anything better to do. The painting was a scene of a woman who looked eerily like I would look twenty years later, sitting under an oak and reading a book. There were so many layers of paint that went over and over the tired white canvas below that it stopped drying completely. There was a half-inch of smelly oils in browns and blues and reds and greens and eventually mostly browns, as all the colors melded together. I stared at her—my creepy future reflection in muddy paints, swirling and changing but always with that same sad expression, unmoved under that tree. After weeks upon weeks of this hobby, all while I was stoned or drunk or both, one night I nonchalantly carried her out to the dumpster in the corner of the apartment complex parking lot and threw her in. I don't remember having a twinge of regret as I walked back to my apartment. I exhaled slowly and watched as my breath looked like dragon smoke in the cool air. I remember distinctly thinking:

"I am wasting my life."

There was one particular afternoon after my brief painting career ended when I was getting high and spending hours staring at the wall (this was before smart phones), that I felt a new uneasiness swell inside of me. It was as if I was floating on a small boat in an ocean with swells the size of skyscrapers around me. I looked to my left and right and I saw nothing but treacherous waves as the rain poured down filling up my shabby boat. I was all alone. And sinking. I walked nervously out of my apartment to my parked car, heard laughter from my neighbors (cringe), and reached for my keys in my purse, making sure the pack of cigarettes and lighter were in there.

I drove to a dead-end road near campus and found my spot on the edge of a hill right behind a church that looked out over the lake. I often came to this one particular grassy knoll (without sounding too cliché), in my sundress in summer or bundled up in soft flannel and sitting on near-freezing ground in late fall, hoping to get some kind of answer from the water or the shore or perhaps someone passing by. I was desperate. Seeking.

The building was grayish-brown stone with a cross that stretched up and over the roof and towered above me. I wondered if that's what it felt like to live in Rio de Janeiro, with the *Christ the Redeemer* by French sculptor Paul Landowski always looming, leering. Quiet.

All at once the tears started to fall and then became sobs that caused my whole body to convulse on that quiet, green hill. How strange I probably looked. How sad. How my onyx-black hair tumbled down my back like a veil of mourning. This was the moment I needed someone to see me. To really see me. To know me. Even though I didn't know it at the time, I was waiting for this knowing, this shared belief or hope that everything was going to be okay.

Something that a mother or father whispers to their child who skins a knee.

Did someone see me? Was someone sitting inside that church building witnessing the shattering? Did they assume that it was God himself who was going to show up to pick up the pieces of me and not God himself through them? As Virginia Woolf noted in her novel, *The Waves*, "on the outskirts of every agony sits some observant fellow who points."

I heard someone say once that if you are on a boat, you aren't going to ask for a life preserver unless you know the ship is going down. Unless, of course, you are on the kind of boat where the captain is responsible and makes everyone wear them and everyone thinks to themselves how awkward that fluorescent orange looks with a bathing suit. For so long I was floating along, doing the bare minimum as a human being, so focused on my own needs—or drowning them—and not seeing anything else. I was so preoccupied with self-medicating and making sure I was anesthetized from any feeling. I did not realize that while I floated on this little wooden boat getting high or drunk and letting the world spin by with gulls circling overhead and the salty smell of sea air all around me, there was a slow leak. I was sinking.

Memory was killing me like a wretched lover that breathes their hideous breath in the morning, noon, night, all hours, and reminded me that I had good reason to want to run from my life:

> Memories that were alive and autonomous, big and small, that approached, single file, suddenly scaling the mattress and invading my body through an ear, or under my fingernails, or through the pores of my skin, until they

entered my brain and battered at it without the slightest pity, with images and moments that my will had wanted never again to recall. And then, when the tribe of memories was still arriving but its presence was becoming less noisy, something else began to invade me with a dreadful coldness, like a rash: the necessity to analyze everything, to find a cause and a reason for everything that had happened in my life [...]. The phase was the worst: the most aggressive, the most tormenting. The one that hurt most. And though I cannot calculate how long it lasted, I do know with absolute certainty that what managed to put an end to it was an unexpected arrival.[13]

It was not until this particular afternoon that I realized for the first time how horrendous my life had become and what a sad state my soul was in. An OG spiritual mystic, Augustine of Hippo, said that "our pilgrimage on earth cannot be exempt from trial. We actually progress by means of trial. We do not know ourselves except through trial, or receive a crown except after victory." I should have known after the trials I had experienced, that a crown was coming (figuratively speaking) but I had no clue who I was. All I knew was that my outsides did not match my insides, as they say in recovery circles. What I was doing in no way lined up with what I valued or what I wanted for my life and future, who I wanted to become. I didn't want to be that girl staring in the mirror hating who she saw staring back at her. I didn't want to be the woman that was so numb to the world around her that she walked through life without being able to feel anything—including the good stuff. That look was getting a little old.

Anxiety, or the more extreme version, panic, is like an emotional storm that blows through and takes away any sense of being able to stand on two feet. The world outside the mind is swirling, heart falling into feet. I've had panic attacks so bad while driving that I have to pull over and force myself not to call 911 for thirty minutes, telling myself that if I die (because panic can make you feel like you are going to die), I die. What triggered it back then? Sometimes it was something familiar: a look, touch, smell. Sometimes it was nothing at all.

Mild anxiety is debilitating, too. I can still function and move about in the world and if someone saw me, I might look crabby or like I have a resting you-know-what face, but that's about it. It's all going on internally. No higher blood pressure, no feeling like the floor is falling out from beneath my feet, no visits to the ER for the EKG test, but still the flitting thoughts take over and don't let anything productive or loving in.

On more than one occasion, near penniless, I remember digging in my jalopy searching for quarters to buy that one last pack of cigarettes or that last bottle of wine even though rent was due and my cell phone fell in the toilet and I had no groceries and the electricity was about to get turned off. Again. I needed something, anything to take the edge off. My fingernails were bitten down to the cuticle and bleeding. There was no way to sift through my list of priorities to figure out what bill I needed to pay because my list of priorities was short. I could fit it folded up in the pocket of my jeans with one line etched in faded pencil: escape.

No friends to call. No one to help.

My life was small. Anxiety, fear (and what I didn't know at the time was shame), kept me in that hidden place where letting anyone else in to my pain would mean opening myself up to being hurt again. There was no way, I thought at the time, that I could survive it. Vulnerability meant weakness. It meant caving. If it had a filter, it was the kind that made everything look like streetlight glow on snow. My fear of people and connection was more than palpable; it became the sun in my life that everything else orbited around.

Addiction has a tendency to strip away everything but the self.

Sometimes we have these unassuming experiences that thunder in our souls and shake the very core of who we are, yet on the outside we look like someone who has allergies. The reality of what goes on in the soul can be so quietly crushing, yet so transformative, it is as if God knows that sometimes these private moments are just for us; these little, ordinary miracle-moments that we only recognize looking back.

A couple weeks later, I was sitting slumped in an uncomfortable gray chair in a thin white hallway, next to a strange woman who said hello. I'd never been to court before, even though I should have, and I was terrified. I couldn't believe that I wound up there, even after all of the choices I never should have made, all of the compromising of my convictions, all of the inebriation, all of the escape. My inability to adult (the verb). Even after the soul-rocking moment sitting on that quiet hill behind the church where my tears fell onto the grass in front of my crossed legs, I couldn't stop. The addictions had gotten their claws into me again and despite how I wanted to change, I just could not do it in my own strength. And now I was facing eviction and homelessness.

To my surprise, this kind woman next to me started asking me questions. She looked me in the eye and asked me my name. Tiny bits of compassion that made little cracks in the shell around my heart. I didn't realize how long I had been waiting for someone to call me by my name and someone safe enough to look in the eye. She was wearing a matching blue track suit and shiny white sneakers and had mousy brown hair pulled back in a bun. She looked comfortable in that space, like she had been there before; and I wondered what an older woman like this was doing in court. And looking so casual about it. I told her about the eviction and about how I knew I was not living the way I was supposed to.

The woman searched me, her blue eyes had softened even more, and said:

"I'm the landlord."

It turned out that she was the one I was going to court with—she had written notices and given me chances and this was it—I was going to be kicked out of my apartment and without shelter.

I should have been evicted and Lord knows the trajectory of my entire life could have been entirely different if she chose to take away my key and the roof over my head (and my cat's) that afternoon. I may have been forced to reach a new bottom, one that could have led me even further into despair. Selling my body or soul. Instead of taking my chance away, she gave me another one.

"I usually don't do this," she said, "but I feel like I'm supposed to help you."

Chapter 5:
THORNS THAT TESTIFY

Give me life, give me pain, give me myself again.
– Tori Amos

My good friend, Emily Killeen, who lives in Arizona and who I met almost a decade ago when I was in early recovery, started a program called Recovery Revival. Emily is super hip, the way I wish I could be, with lovely golden mermaid hair, super cute yoga clothes and a picture-perfect life on a small off-grid homestead in Northern Arizona. I agreed to be a part of the three-month program with women in all stages of the recovery journey, from sober curious to long-term recovery to "happy, sober and free" (Emily's favorite saying). We were about a month into the program, which consisted of daily gratitude journaling, movement and other exercises, and meeting weekly for a couple hours on Zoom, when Emily announced during one of our meetings that we would be working on our "timelines." We needed to prepare sharing our stories around this format, all eight of us in one evening, including her: the good and bad and ugly of what had happened to us and what we had done.

I had written out my timeline before, reminiscent of homework I did during adolescent addiction treatment. But this time it was different because I was nine years and some change in recovery and even more years struggling, off and on, to attain it. When my timeline was completed, I realized that I hadn't shared my full story like that in a long time – if ever. Bits and pieces to friends and at meetings and to my husband and whispered to God (who already knew it all anyways) but that was it, never the whole thing in one Sharpie-decorated one-pager.

I took my time, interchanging a rainbow of colors and drawing hearts and smiley faces and clouds with rain drops and lightning—like the doodles on my sixth-grade math folder. After each section—teens, twenties, thirties—I got up and shook it off (like I do during online YouTube yoga), got a cup of tea and a salty snack and came back. When I was done, I stared at it: my life's main events in a series of small etches on a short line. I wondered to myself how ridiculous it would be if such things were done "out there," outside of recovery circles.

What if my small group at church or the Sunday school that my husband and I lead asked people to do this?

"Okay, Christians, get your markers out. It's time to make a list of every horrible thing done to you and everything you've never told anyone out loud. That sexual assault in college—that you did—write it down and tell us. That divorce? We want all the gritty details of all the ways he never showed up for you. Stealing in high school? Those candy bars from the corner store? Line them up. How you fantasize about that woman in front of you in the pews? What's her name?"

There are so many books in the Christian market that need to be in the everyone market. I'm just saying. One author I met and fell in love with instantly after I learned that he was a Catholic priest who was also a drunk who was also in recovery who also left the priesthood to get married, is the late Brennan Manning. Brennan, like many of his contemporaries, have a habit of repeating the same (good) stories because they are good.

The one he tells in his famous book *Ragamuffin Gospel* and again in his autobiography, *All Is Grace: A Ragamuffin Memoir*, is about a man named Max that he meets in addiction treatment at Hazelden. Max is ruthlessly questioned in the hotseat of group therapy, sitting, all eyes, in the middle of an open circle. The uncomfortableness is palpable. It tastes like mouthwash or vanilla extract straight up. The therapist and the other men in the treatment group are allowed to ask him tough questions.

This isn't your average church small group. It's more like group confession—unwilling confession. Manning recalls how Max was smug, quoting Bible verses about eyes and planks. He refused to acknowledge that his drinking was a problem. The counselor, exasperated, calls Max's family in front of the group to get their perspective on this question: "Have you ever been unkind to your children?"

Max's wife recounts a time when Max was supposed to drive his daughter home, but instead stops at a bar on his way and leaves his daughter in the car, off, in freezing, sub-zero temperatures.

His daughter's ears and fingers were badly frostbitten, resulting in the need for amputation of a thumb and permanent hearing loss. Max collapsed on all fours and began to sob, reduced to the ground of his lies and deceptions.[14]

All at once his veil of togetherness was torn. Nothing stood in the way of Max and the lie he held onto: that his drinking wasn't a problem. In that weary room of addiction treatment, the counselor and all of the men witnessed a radical moment of need that transformed into a radical moment of redemption. Manning wished he had that experience. He longed to break as Max had.

I've seen this replayed time and again in the dark basements of recovery circles. And that night with the group of women on my laptop screen, sharing their secrets and vulnerabilities, I was reminded of this cathartic breaking that Brennan Manning had witnessed and so eloquently captured for me to read decades later.

The only word that I can think of to describe the sharing from that night is heavy. Not heavy like a box of books is heavy, heavy like the Titanic. I thought that *my* story was traumatic. What I saw and heard on that Zoom call with eight women from around the country and one in Australia (hey, mate!), I will never forget.

Woman after woman shared the details of abuses, rapes, deaths, divorces, abandonment, substance use, overdoses, seeking, using and being used. It was a tidal wave of suffering, the kind of suffering that can only be felt by those who have been subjected unwillingly to it. I closed my eyes after one of the shares, a woman retelling in vivid detail about finding her young mother dead. What it felt like, looked like, smelled like: blue skin and empty, open eyes. Then another young woman sharing about how her good friend's father got her drunk, kissed her with his stale mouth and raped her. And then how it happened again by a good friend's husband. And another woman who woke up in a strange country to find her boyfriend dead in the bed next to her with a needle still hanging in his arm.

After the meeting ended, what kept going through my mind was pieces of my past, like mosaic glass, jagged, piercing. I thought about that time in college, dabbling in another creative pursuit, when I tried arranging and rearranging pieces of broken glass on wood, getting glass dust in the pads of my fingers and that soft, fleshy part that someone holds if they are going to read your palm. It had been a while since I felt my stories sting and the pain of it cutting me again and again. The drugs and alcohol and drowning sorrows. The men. The no's and the silence. It had been over ten years ago, yet these images flitted back and forth and mingled with the other women's stories so much that I could not separate the pain from their experiences and my own. It was like I was sitting in one huge pot of bubbling, stinky brokenness and I was melting from the outside in.

After the virtual meeting, I went outside on our back porch and looked up at the night sky. The stars were bright and I could see one that was very large and had a reddish tint, maybe Mars. The air smelled like summer ending. It was cool for the South and the blackness of the sky melted in to the blackness of the woods around us. I heard an owl screech like a child, followed by a *who-who-who*. And then it came to mind as quickly as the sound of the owl had come and gone: I recalled a scene from the Bible when Jesus wept bitterly over a friend who had died.

The verse "Jesus wept" is actually the shortest verse in all of scripture.[15] Jon Bloom, staff writer for desiringGod.org, says that this short passage shows how God is sympathetic with our suffering and the picture of Jesus at the tomb of Lazarus gives us insight into "how the Father feels over the affliction and grief his children's experience."[16] In other words, we have a God who is compassionate because He has been there.[17]

Jesus wept.

Now, trust me, there would have been a time in my life when someone said all of this stuff to me about Jesus being there and crying with me and that God understands because he has walked through everything I have and blah, blah, blah. I would have heard all of this and said, "yeah right," or more likely, I would have stared back and nodded in agreement, but thought silently to myself: *Yeah right*. Jesus wasn't a woman.

When you are a woman in the thick of the wilderness, trust me— sometimes the last thing you want or need to hear is a theology lesson. When you have experienced things that make you doubt not only

God's love but the very existence of a higher power, it takes more than a sermon to let the truth sink in.

I stared into the night. I love how the stars and moon, reflecting light, brighten up the woods around us. I saw the individual trees and shrubs and stone. When I looked past the blackness, I saw that it was not just darkness. There was form around me. There was meaning. I thought about how the God I had come to know had cried so much for me and for all of these women who lived lives of such brokenness and pain. In the coolness of the night, I felt a warm embrace around me again just like I had at different points along the way. This warm embrace spoke: it's going to be ok. It was the same embrace that helped my heart melt bit by bit over the years.

I cried.

Sometimes when I am watching cartoons (something educational—do not judge) with my kiddos, my son will be standing and watching in front of me and slowly back up until he knows he can sit down. Without turning around to confirm that I am still there, he trusts wholly and completely that I am. He sits down into my lap with a smile like a child who feels completely content, completely safe, completely free to fall into me.

During my years of struggle, (and if I'm honest, sometimes today) I desire to have a relationship with God like that. Like those moments with my son. Like someone who believes what sermons say about the love of Jesus and that God has actually been through the hard stuff with us. There were so many times I wished I could have sat down into God's lap with a smile, knowing that, no matter what, he was there for me and waiting, expectant. Hebrews 11:1 says that "faith is confidence in what we hope for and assurance about what we do not see." Just like my son, there were times in my past that I wanted to back up and know that when I sat down, I'd be sitting in my daddy's lap. As I stared out at the southern night and listened to the crickets and other strange insects sing their content songs, I thought about how hard, yet how necessary, that trust fall is.

I sent a text to one of the women who, with courage, shared at the virtual meeting about her own rape and sexual abuse as a child.

"How are you doing? That was heavy tonight."

"I'm okay," she said.

I could feel the weight she held, too, the weight she longed to set down. She wasn't a Christian, but she knew I was. She knew when I told them all that night the reason that I hoped and what I believed finally set me free. It wasn't just something I said with my mouth. It was a heart-truth, one I felt with my body and soul, that luminescent part that carries all of our experiences, the lovely and the hard, and creates something of purpose from it.

"Even when I'm not okay, like tonight. Like when I feel almost buried under the pain that so many of us have experienced, I know it doesn't have to be dark. We can live lit up."

She laughed.

"In the good way."

Chapter 6:
ONE IS NEVER ENOUGH

I just want to sleep. A coma would be nice. Or amnesia. Anything,
just to get rid of this, these thoughts, whispers in my mind.
— Laurie Halse Anderson

S unlight cascaded down around the hillsides, in between swaying branches and the June corn, while Chloe and I drank our
strawberry wine and smoked Marlboro cigarettes, flying like
birds in the back of pickups. It must have looked like an Aerosmith
music video as we rode through psalm-green hills. We raised our arms
in the air as the truck twisted around bends in the countryside. I
closed my eyes and let the wind dance around my new curves. When
I was drinking, I felt free, like anything was possible.

Alcohol instantly gave me a warm feeling like a friend welcoming
me home. It tingled as it worked its way through my body and made
me feel content in my own skin. First, I felt a rushing glow overwhelm
me, and then my head felt as light as the summer sky around us. I
was confident and pretty. I said all the right things and wrong things

when I was supposed to. I was everything I wasn't when I was sober. Adolescent insecurity vanished and I fell in love with the way, with each sip, I could inch further away from what I was actually feeling, further from myself.

In recovery circles, after you've been around for a while, you start to hear some of the same things repeated. Stories about what it was like in active addiction and how the first time or couple of times or even for some, the first few years or even decades of using alcohol or other drugs, brings an answer to a very important question we'd been asking for a long time.

"Belonging."

"Warm feeling."

"Something clicked."

"Found what I had been looking for."

"Finally made sense."

"Became who I wanted to be."

The first times getting drunk, for me, were idyllic and I spent years chasing these highs. All of those things I heard among my recovery friends were true for me. It was like something clicked. The strong desire to escape who I was and how I felt, even at such a young age—this I could finally do through drinking. I had my answer. Or as I saw written on a meme: "I used to think drinking was bad for me, so I gave up thinking."

The good times didn't roll along for too long. The picture-perfect scenes and feelings—it all got muddier sooner than I would have chosen. The next couple of times I got drunk as a tween, my lack of control was more than apparent. I knew right away that I did not drink like everyone else. After I had one drink, it was all over. At thirteen, I knew that I was an alcoholic.

The summer after eighth grade, a good friend of my stepmom's asked me to babysit and I agreed, feeling pretty good about my barely teenage self right before high school started. I was such a grown-up now (how hysterical when you actually see what a thirteen-year-old looks like today) and this only proved it to me even more. The girl I was babysitting was almost as old as me. She wanted to go to a friend's house, which was OK'd by her mother. So, one late summer afternoon, I was alone in a house. I decided to do what most teenagers with blossoming alcoholism are inclined to do: I looked around. There was a full liquor cabinet. After a couple hushed phone calls to girls on landlines (this was long before cell phones), who called a couple boys, the good idea was about to start.

We mixed all sorts of crazy concoctions together: vodka and gin and crème de menthe and Captain Morgan. Then we poured it over a splash of Mountain Dew and old, freezer burnt ice cubes. Time warped as it does in a semi-blackout and all I remember is drinking the thick and sickeningly sweet mixture, French kissing a boy with braces under the stairs and then hearing "Someone's coming!" Everyone scattered.

The walls spun and I fell trying to climb back up the stairs. In an instant, there I was alone and drunk out of my mind. A scene that would replay countless times after that day. It was the girl's older brother who eventually opened the door and stared at me as I tried to hold myself up by the kitchen sink. He knew right away what had happened when he saw the bottles and half-drunk cups and smelled the sweet ethanol. I stumbled around and pleaded with him not to tell my parents. He drove me home in his blue Camaro as I held my head out the window and puked fluorescent-orange onto the side of his car.

Somehow, surprisingly, I sobered up enough by the time my parents got home. My brother helped me into the shower fully clothed and made me drink coffee and eat chunks of bread like he'd seen on movies. I came down for dinner, talking quietly when asked a question ("yes, babysitting went well"). Of course, they would find out the next day when the girl's mother called and I would have to pay back my stepmom's friend for the booze and it would be years before my parents would trust me again. This moment unleashed a series of lies I would come to rely on to be able to leave the house to drink; the ones I needed to drink and use like I thought I needed to.

Any sane person would have stopped after this babysitting misadventure (to put it mildly), but it was only the beginning for me. Looking back now I can see the insanity clear as the breeze: the lying, the need and compulsion to drink. Sneaking beers from my family's fridge and waiting in the woods near the road in the middle of the night for someone to pick me up in a pickup truck with a 12-pack. I see a thirteen-year-old girl today and see how young she looks, how naïve and innocent and in need of someone to protect her she is; how she should still be playing with toys and pretending to dress up with her mother's makeup. Not playing adult so soon and way too young to be playing alcoholic.

The places a young girl can go in the middle of the night to get drunk are not very wholesome. Think the opposite of church youth group. It was exhausting trying to figure out how to sneak a phone into my bedroom to make those calls (again, this was BC or before cell phones); or how to walk quietly past two sleeping dogs, unlock the back door and walk through the dark on a leaf covered path with the smell of beer and vanilla perfume and hairspray following me into the car that crept up with headlights off; or how to slink in the back door, change my shirt and wipe away the mascara stains before hopping on the bus to sneak another beer—or if I was lucky Vodka—before class.

One of the places I stole away to was a little side room of a house on someone's farm. I'm still not sure what this building was used for in the daylight, but there was a couch and TV and fridge and a cement ledge where us girls could sit and smoke our stinky cigarettes and chug our cheap beers and kick our legs back and forth with our white lacey socks and keep up with the boys. Most of the other people who met late at night were like me, I am sure; why else on a Tuesday night at 2:00 a.m. would we all be utterly wasted at fourteen and sixteen and seventeen instead of at home asleep, dreaming of the things teens should be dreaming about?

Not surprisingly, I started dating a boy who was a senior. His name was Ben and he drove a huge Cadillac and picked me up on the side of the road (I realize how this sounds) and we drank our Bud Light and listened to Tim McGraw and Deana Carter and made-out in a bedroom that had posters of a bikini-clad Cindy Crawford and dusty NASCAR memorabilia. We got drunk most nights of the week and I learned early on that as a woman, the rule of the guy paying for stuff was nice when you are an alcoholic.

I knew I was an alcoholic right away. I knew it when I road tripped with Chloe and strawberry wine; I knew it the nights I'd sneak out and go to school still drunk; I knew it once I realized I didn't have an off switch and once I started doing things that were not like me: lying to my parents, for example. I knew I was an alcoholic after getting puking drunk after babysitting and when I started going out with Ben. I knew I was an alcoholic when I had to lie, even at such a young age, to cover up my drinking.

Sometimes I was "at a friend's" and sometimes I was "out in the woods for a walk" but just getting home from the party the night before. There were cornfield parties that were the "movies." I even pretended to be in track and field one spring, complete with practicing every day when all this really meant was that I was in some boy's attic smoking cigarettes and drinking vodka and watching a bunch of stoners play 007 on a PlayStation.

The lies—like the drinking—worked for a time, until it didn't. Until I needed more and more and the alcohol wasn't as convenient or strong enough. I needed to fall further away from myself.

Rise Together is an amazing organization that supports healthy youth development.[18] I've seen Nadine Machkovech, one of its founders and a wellness coach, and her team speak on numerous occasions, standing-room only, with moms who've lost children to opioid overdose or alcohol addiction. One mom used to bring her daughter's ashes in a bright pink urn and sit it on the podium when she spoke with them. It was not like any high school speaking program that I remember—or don't remember—from high school. They speak directly to teens' insecurities and pain by sharing their own experience. They connect by getting real about the dark places they've been: addiction, suicidal ideation, never feeling good enough, anxiety, depression, and body image issues. I've followed Rise Together on social media for years and it's always amazing to see the panoramic photographs of Nadine standing, stylishly dressed with holey jeans, a fresh balayage and bright white t-shirt that says: THE FUTURE IS YOUTH in front of thousands of students who are hanging on every word like she has the answer to some question they've been asking for years.

Nadine has a TedTalk called "The Secret to Being Enough."[19] In it she states passionately, "either the drugs were going to take me or I was going to end it all, myself. I was so ashamed." She reminds her audience that her story of rock bottom at age seventeen, too, was nothing unique, that one in three households in the United States deals with addiction issues of some kind. She was just one of millions of young people that began masking mental health issues, trauma, and other insecurities with alcohol and other drugs. In her talk, Nadine confesses that a secret she hid was that she never felt good enough; her problems did not start with addiction. Then, by the time she reached high school, "'just say no' wasn't just that easy." I could relate. Ever since I looked into my grandfather's mirror and hated what I saw, ever since I started sneaking those beers and then lying and sneaking around some more, I knew that something was wrong.

I could not shake the sense that I was missing something. Everything was not okay.

I walked down the hallways my freshman year and the sneers and the calls of "fresh meat" were dizzying. The feeling of not being enough continued. The feeling that I didn't belong continued. The growing desire to escape it all intensified and the drinking continued. Looking back now I wish someone would have warned me. I wish someone would have told me to be careful.

Chapter 7:
STINGS ON ITS WAY DOWN

There was a star riding through clouds one night
& I said to the star, 'Consume me'.
– Virginia Woolf

Ashley had cherub cheeks, the kind that women in their fifties, losing their elasticity, pay thousands of dollars to re-create, but never capture. Her chocolate eyes and purple-brown hair, her smiling, lip-glossed mouth, her innocent laugh—all of these pieces of her I wonder about when I think about what happened.

She was one of a handful of students in recovery that frequented recovery meetings, becoming by default a darling of recovery. Young women like her became your little sister or daughter, innocence that needed protecting, because with the years came an understanding that for us girls, things only get harder when you are an alcoholic or addict.

She liked to smoke the same cigarettes I did so we became fast friends. Ashley told me about her home life. The trailer that she was embarrassed of on the other side of the tracks. How hard it was that

Christmases never came and birthdays went by unnoticed so that by high school, she and her siblings weren't really sure anymore when the days actually were. She had adopted June 14th as her day and she would steal Laffy Taffy candy from the gas station and sit on the edge of her bed and dream about new, shiny things.

As she puffed smoke out her nostrils like I used to do at that age, she told me stories about her friends at the alternative high school.

"It's for druggies like me," she'd say and I'd correct her, unable to stomach the harmful words she used to talk about herself.

"Billy is such a jerk. He pulls my hair from the seat behind me like he's twelve or something. Carly is like a total drama queen, but whatever. She's always trying to get me to hang out with these older guys who are super creepy."

Ashley and I went to meetings for a while and I listened as she talked about school and boys and clothes and how it was hard growing up poor. And even harder being a teen in addiction recovery.

"Everyone smokes pot. Like everyone. It's not really even considered a drug anymore."

Then one day she was gone.

I saw on my Facebook feed the missing child photograph with her rose cheeks and smiling eyes. I couldn't believe it and kept staring at the photo, clicking the link, re-reading every word. Gone? Ashley is missing for 24 hours and if anyone knows of her whereabouts, we need to call this number? My eyes froze on hers in the picture and I imagined the worst. Ashley, so young and naïve, so prone to insecurity and that dangerous hunger for affection and love that I knew well.

The days turned into weeks and I learned after contacting the school what the police think happened. One of the other girls at the alternative school was a recruiter for a prostitution ring in the city. The police and other authorities were investigating. It had happened before to other girls. They lure them with money and clothes and cell phones. Ashley was last spotted outside a hotel near a prominent highway in the city.

My heart ached for her. And I, with the imagination of a screenplay writer, mentally enacted every possible scenario. I thought of the time when my dad made me watch the movie *Taken* with Liam Neeson after I told him I wanted to go backpacking in Europe when I was nineteen. Did she go willingly? Was she drugged? Was she being held against her will? If the police knew where she was, why weren't they rescuing her? Why wasn't someone doing something?

I called and spoke to the director of the school several times and always the same answer:

"They are working on bringing her home."

Every day that went by, the thought of Ashley followed me.

Then one day she was back.

Ashley walked into the meeting room and slumped in a chair near the exit. Her once bubbly eyes were sunken, with dark purple circles outlining them like floating half-moons. I was ecstatic and could barely stay in my seat. I noticed as each person shared or said "pass" and some cried as they opened up for the first time and proclaimed out loud "...and I'm an alcoholic" that Ashley remained unmoved. Her gaze steady on the floor in front of her. As soon as the meeting ended, I bolted to her and waited as other women who recognized her wanted to say hello, too. There are no strangers in recovery spaces.

"Do you need a ride?" I asked, hoping that she did.

She nodded and walked with me silently to the car. She asked for a smoke and we drove away from the meeting space with men and women still lingering together like moths around a porch light on a summer night.

"We missed you."

Ashley let out a little laugh and then started to cry. I asked her if she felt comfortable talking about what happened and bit by bit, from her stops and starts and what I recognize now as disassociating, she told me what happened.

"They had a lot of us in that hotel. The whole floor. Every room."

I inhaled deeply and tried to focus on the road as she continued. I looked over and saw that she was shaking.

"I'm not sure how I got there, but once I was in that bed, I couldn't leave. I think they drugged me or something."

Ashley went on until we pulled into her driveway and the shadow of the metal roof of the trailer cast an eerie glow over her.

I did what they say to do in situation like that. I listened. I made sure she didn't have a plan for harming herself. I made sure she had supports in place like therapy to deal with the trauma of what she had experienced. I asked her if there was anything else that I could do, if she wanted to stay with me. If her mom was home. I asked her if she was okay. If she was going to be okay.

"Yeah, I'm okay."

I wasn't sure she was and definitely wasn't sure I was going to be. I saw the outline of her mother in the window, pulling the curtain aside, making sure it was me.

As I drove off, I prayed. I asked God to help Ashley the way he had helped me. I prayed hard for the shame of whatever Ashley had experienced to be lifted and carried away. I cried all the way home as I thought about how many Ashley's and Carly's and Caroline's there are who are violated and abused and taken in different ways.

The following week, Ashley disappeared again. And never came back.

After another school year faded into summer and my junior year swam by, my dad gave me an ultimatum on a humid afternoon: either go to addiction treatment or you are going into foster care. By then

I had moved into a dingy apartment in the small town where I lived. It had ramen noodles left in sauce pans in the sink, beer cans and wine bottles with sticks of burnt incense and cigarette butts floating in them. Two older girls lived there who recently graduated and it was my only option after moving in with my mother didn't work (my parents were divorced) and staying with my dad and stepmom continued to be a struggle because of my desperate lies and attempts to cover up my using.

Occasionally, I tried to do things like go to dances or to the movies—normal teenage stuff—but the desire was too strong. I ended up in the backseat of a dealer's car blowing my nose in an old shirt, trying to stop the bleeding so I could snort a line. Word got around as it often does in high school. Not only was I a "slut" and "whore" (*I can't believe she had sex with him in the bathroom of that party!*) now I was a "druggie." Loser. Burn-out.

I crashed into other drugs like meth—a little here and there when I couldn't find any coke (I say that now like it's something I "dabbled in," like classical piano). For a couple weeks my junior year, I had burnt fingertips and my baggy sweatshirts smelled like metallic smoke. I'd have friends over, or people who I thought were my friends, and we listened to songs on repeat and hollowed out our minds, talking about who knows what for who knows how long. I still can't believe I ever thought any of this was fun. Or that I made it out alive to tell the story.

What these harder drugs did do was help me to numb myself even more. The anxiety, the depression, the flashbacks—all of it was able to fade away (at least for a time) until the effects wore off and I was in another desperate search for something else to make it all go away. I can still remember the desperate ways that I tried to find drugs if I was out or if I knew I would be needing something soon. While I didn't have to resort to selling my body like many get trapped into, I always seemed to know how to find and fall in love with people who sold drugs. I could ride along and get high like I was a blonde and puffy Penelope Cruz in *Blow*. It wasn't so much a business transaction as an exchange.

I'm not proud of any of this and really, it has taken me years to get to a place where I can share this part of my story straight-faced and without that little patch of skin on my neck turning red. The things I've done should have either killed me or at least given me a lengthy prison stay. But as they say in recovery circles—and one of the many one-liners that I truly love— "our secrets keep us sick." That's why I'm sharing it all with you.

A part of me was relieved when I got the ultimatum from my dad. Finally, it was black or white: go to treatment or we are done with you. There was no way I wanted to go into foster care with less than a year until I turned eighteen. I knew in what was left of my heart that I needed out.

Chapter 8:

BEAUTY FROM THE ASH HEAP

Let me hear joy and gladness;
let the bones you have crushed rejoice.
— Psalm 51:8

n recovery, part of the healing process includes sharing our stories. You might be familiar with recovery meetings, or perhaps you know someone or have yourself attended a support group of some kind, whether it was for cancer, grief or divorce. Name your issue and there is probably a 12 or 13-step (inside joke here) program for you. What is similar about various kinds of support groups is that for almost all of them, sharing is a large part of what goes on. That and drinking coffee or smoking cigarettes or vaping, if you frequent the kind that I am familiar with.

Recovery isn't a place that you can show up to silent. There are no worship bands or liturgies. No sermons or benedictions. What is there? Time and space. There is a place to show up. To let it out. To give those dark parts no more time to be hidden. Confession is something that happens publicly, not with a bowed head and not behind the curtain. Our mess has the lead solo. And everyone is listening. The music is honesty. The liturgy is a list of character defects. The sermon is a soliloquy. The benediction is a prayer shared. Out loud.

There is an unspoken and sometimes spoken format that shares can follow: what it was like, what happened and what it's like now. I like this because as a writer, I like organization. I like things to flow, to be structured, to make sense; I like to know what to expect. Like the psalmists, there are also shares of gratitude and joy that over-floweth! Then, there are the utterances of despair and rejection like the cries of only those who have experienced things like addiction and trauma can relate to: the full-on manic back and forth of the human experience. Joy and pain. Triumph and defeat. Beauty and disgust. Love and death.

I met Anne Lamott when a friend gave me a copy of *Bird by Bird*, her practical and whimsical guide to writing. After falling in love with the book and doing a little Google research, I was shocked to find out that she, too, is a Christian, one that talks openly about things like yelling at her child, despising her cellulite, and resting erratically and irreverently on her addiction recovery. Anne has a way with thoughts that makes her feel like a soul-friend, not someone you'd necessarily bring home to meet your parents, but the kind of friend you tell all your secrets to.

Anne wrote another book called *Plan B: Further Thoughts on Faith* and tells a story about the time she went to the San Quentin prison to teach creative writing to prisoners with another member of her church, Neshama. Lamott writes:

> Jesus had an affinity for prisoners. He had been one, after all. He must have often felt anxiety and isolation in jail, but

he always identified with the prisoners. He made a point of befriending the worst and most hated, because his message was that no one was beyond the reach of divine love, despite society's way of stating the opposite. God: what a nut."[20]

She goes on to talk about what it was like to enter the prison, walk down the dimly lit corridors, imagining the worst. Prison breaks of a *Shawshank Redemption* variety, forced conjugal visits. She then shares what happened after her friend, Neshama, told the prisoners a story. The prisoners were surprised, expecting to be talked at or preached to. Instead, Neshama entertained with a story about a man who missed some good things in life because he was too focused on himself. The prisoners' "faces lit up with surprise. She was shining on them, and they felt her shining on them, and so they shone back on her."[21]

It had been a long time since many of these prisoners, most serving life sentences for murder, heard an uplifting, moral-invoking story. Anne continues:

> They asked her questions. Where do we find these stories? And Neshama told them: "They're in you, like jewels in your hearts." Why do they matter? "Because they're treasures. These memories, these images, come forth from the ground of the same wisdom we all know, but that you alone can tell."[22]

The same is true about telling our recovery stories, the real versions. The X-rated and shame-laden and gag reflex-inducing stories. Also, the ones with heart-smushing grief like the stories that Ashley told and the joy only someone who is seeing the world for the first time—again—knows about.

I've noticed that when I share my story these days, I focus mostly on the "what it's like now" part of the equation. The "what it was like" feels far away, most days. A hundred years ago. But part of why I let all of you into this secret place now is because I know I need to be reminded of the past. Not to stay there; do not misunderstand me. It's to remember where I have come from, what I have come through and what I could lose if I ever decided to go back. If I ever decide that wandering in the desert again is a better use of my time than sun-bathing in the Promised Land. When the things buried deep in our hearts and minds come into the light, something miraculous can happen.

I went to inpatient treatment for the first time that summer before my senior year in high school and started learning about my addiction. It was exhilarating. I drank in everything I was learning, especially the science of addiction. The more I listened, the more I realized that maybe it was not about me being "bad," maybe I had some type of genetic predisposition, something in my family that brought addiction closer. One of the women I met in Recovery Revival said that she likes to think of addiction like a path in the woods. When you take the same route over and over again, the path becomes more worn and it is easier to get from point A to point B. It also becomes automatic; you don't have to look down anymore, because you know the way is clear. There are no leaves to brush away or logs to step over. Similarly, the more and more you use substances, the more this pathway in your brain becomes so worn that you end up thinking this is the only way to go. Getting sober is like having to clear a new path in an overgrown forest, something straight out of *Lord of the Rings*—walking through the seemingly impossible, with machete in hand, over and over again until something that resembles a thin break in the thick of things starts to emerge.

My good friend, Florence Hilliard, has traveled for decades nationally to speak about the science of addiction and recovery. In one of her trainings, Florence talks about how powerful the brain that God gave us really is. Think about this: imagine you are slicing into a ripe and juicy lemon…

Is your mouth watering already, the sides of your cheeks puckering as if you'd already bitten into that sour thing and you have to take a sip of water to get all that citrus out? That is the power of suggestion and of how the brain responds to triggers. You know that a lemon is sour and that if you bite into it, well, here my mouth goes again responding to my brain firing: "Warning! Sour! EEK! You better start salivating now!" This gives you a glimpse of just how powerful the brain can be. Imagine how hard it is for someone to clear a new pathway and start re-teaching the brain that it doesn't need substances. I learned in treatment that there was a reason I had all these "triggers" that seemed too powerful for me to withstand. There was a reason I could not control the strong desire I had to use once the thought got lodged in my brain. Once I saw it, felt it, tasted it, heard it—it was almost impossible to escape.

The word "addiction" actually comes from a Latin root that means "enslaved by" or bound to" (for all of my word-nerds out there: interesting connection to the root of the word for stigma, no?). It has taken society a long time to realize that addiction is not some moral failing or weakness (although clearly there is a spiritual component to all of this), but a reaction of the brain that occurs in some people and it is a medical condition like any other—like heart disease, diabetes or cancer. According to some smart people at Harvard: "Addiction exerts a long and powerful influence on the brain that manifests in three distinct ways: craving for the object of addiction, loss of control over its use, and continuing involvement with it despite adverse consequences."[23]

In other words, addiction literally "hijacks" the brain. It changes the brain's functioning by "subverting the way it registers pleasure and then by corrupting other normal drives such as learning and motivation."[24] The Apostle Paul gave other words, a bit less scientific, to the phenomenon when he described in Romans 7 about what it is like to be human and enslaved by sin: "I do not understand what I do. For what I want to do I do not do, but what I hate I do."[25]

The Apostle Paul struggled with the reality of being human and in need of help, and this fits the concept of addiction perfectly. Perhaps Paul even knew of someone who struggled with addiction or addictive tendencies. Or perhaps he, too, knew what it felt like to be alone with a silent struggle, one eating him from the inside out.

What is really interesting to note is that it is not just alcohol and other drugs that can "hijack" the brain and enslave it. Shopping, scrolling, eating, gambling, playing video games, looking at pornography—all of these actions have been found to change the way the brain functions. These actions can literally rewire the brain. God created this small, three-pound gray and pretty gross organ to be the place where loving thoughts come from, where grand ideas are born and new inventions created, and also where someone like me can get lost in impenetrable darkness.

Along with learning more about addiction and my spiritual condition in treatment, I was able to meet other young people going through what I was going through: other teens with parents who were "so over the top" and "controlling" and who wouldn't let us "do what we wanted." One of the women there, Lily, was tall and had long brown hair and talked about her bulimia and cocaine problem like she was discussing what dress she was going to wear for the prom. We hit it off right away. We were all tattered and shaky and smelling of smoke and Bath and Body Works Sweet Pea lotion. We still slept with teddy bears and exchanged stories of our sexual assaults. We were excited to change and terrified at the same time—mostly because we knew we had to face our friends and school when we got home.

My counselor, Richard, was a gentle older man with long wavy gray hair and circular glasses, who loved to wear polo shirts and had a small Native American wedding vase in his office that I loved to look at and wonder what types of flowers they put in either side of the vase way back when. I don't recall much of what we talked about or what he said during these meetings except for one particular meeting on one particular day when he looked me in the eyes and said:

"Your life has purpose and value."

A.W. Tozer in *The Crucified Life* says that "the prevailing question is, what is God's purpose in our lives? The answer to that one question will open up a whole world of understanding concerning what God is doing in our circumstances."[26] By the time I reached Richard's office and sat slumped in that office chair, staring at the impressionist treatment art, wondering about that black and reddish-brown vase, my purpose felt far away. I had lost it. I knew I needed to get to the point where I was ready to ask that question and believe that I was worthy of an answer. Richard's comment planted a seed in my heart:

I was worth saving.

I left inpatient treatment with a binder full of drawings and scribbles on the recovery steps and what songs were triggers and what to do if I got asked to use again. I wrote a poem about the demon on my shoulder; and in my pocket, I carried a small shell with the names of four kids on it, all four of us from the adolescent unit who had scribbled our names in marker and exchanged them. I still have mine in a small red velvet box that I hope to tell my kids about someday.

My intentions were good when I left the safety of treatment. I wanted to be sober. The predictability of the routine and the supportive hugs and nods and "I get it" affirmations from the other kids there were powerful; treatment was a safe place. A place where shame didn't need to live in hiding because we all knew her. Returning to my old friends and boyfriend was not safe. How could they have been? They were struggling with their own addictions and insecurities and quiet adolescent sufferings. Plus, girls can be cruel. As much as we now want to lift each other up, pray for each other and sign up for the meal train when new babies are born or when loved one's pass, high school girls can be hurtful in ways that can harm you for eternity. I have sat across from countless people in recovery meetings that talk about the invisible scars left from their own experiences of being bullied.

After I left treatment, the first day of school I walked down the hallway full of excitement. I wasn't afraid of the other girls. My mind was fresh and clear; I showered and cared what I put on for clothes: a new pale-yellow zip up with a butterfly and dark jeans that were a couple sizes closer to my normal size. I got up an hour early to curl my long, freshly dyed blonde hair. Things were going to be different. I was a senior. I saw Chloe standing with a small circle of other girls. They were laughing and talking and all looking genuinely happy. I walked past them and smiled. They smiled back.

I found my locker. That feeling I usually had like everyone was watching me was completely gone. It was as if I was a little less inside of my head and a little more present. After getting the books I needed and hanging my bag on its hook, I smoothed my hair down over my ear and took a big deep breath. Turning, I caught eyes with one of the boys in my grade, one who looked like him. Short, wearing an over-sized sky-blue t-shirt. Something started to feel strange.

I have a friend call it "the swoosh"—an anxious flush of energy and blood and nerves. I breathed again and pictured Richard's face. His soft eyes. Then Lily's. I laughed to myself when I thought about the way that Lily pretended to say hi to me with her little red teddy bear before the lights got turned off for the night. The smell of her perfume: Vanilla Sky. I missed her and I missed everything about treatment. I missed the way it smelled oddly comforting like a freshly cleaned hospital room. I missed the predictability and the way that we were safe there in our sober bubble. Nothing could harm us.

I turned again down the cavernous hall and walked through the doors of my first class and behind me I heard something, faint at first and then louder as they approached:

"Crackhead."

"Loser."

"Junkie."

It was not long before I was sitting in the passenger seat rolling up a joint and passing it to the back seat, feeling the loud bass of the music in my bones again as the seat shook beneath me. The ultimatum from my dad, treatment and Lily, the shell and Richard, everything I had learned felt far away, like memories of running along a beach as a child. It was not long until someone in the backseat had a little fold of paper like an origami sailboat and "one line of cocaine" wasn't going to hurt anyone, I told myself. But one turned into too many, turned into never enough, and again my relationship with substances melded into that desperate place as if I never experienced the lovely taste of recovery at all.

What I remember next?

The crash and the absence of God.

The anger at God.

When you are coming down off of a cocaine binge it feels like you got hit by a train, one of the really fast ones. My limbs grew so heavy it was as if the blood circulating in them was cement; I could not get up off the couch and the tears fell, incessant. The depression, like a weighted blanket, covered me so completely that it was hard to see beyond it. Even taking other substances: MDMA or ecstasy, meth, mushrooms, even huffing lighter fluid—nothing worked to help me get back to that place of peace I was searching for so frantically. The truth was that it was a long time since any of it had made me feel like the first time, made me feel like myself. What I was looking for was always just out of reach.

By seventeen, my brain needed drugs just to feel normal. I learned in treatment how cocaine and other drugs, including alcohol, create a false sense of "happiness" through a hefty dopamine release. Over time, because this dopamine is artificially made and triggered by outside substances, the brain stops naturally producing it. I did not want to remember that as a person who is addicted, my brain now needed this substance to function normally and release the chemicals it would normally do in a person who does not use, just to make me feel okay. Despite countless failed attempts after treatment to stop using again, nothing worked. Every day I woke up to stare down the tracks at another train coming my way.

Then the night it was all over, the night I have no solid memory, only fragments of a scene where I am looking out a window in front of me, while leaning against the wall, waiting for the ambulance. Snow fell quietly and I had an eerie sense that I was supposed to be right where I was, though I had no recollection of what had happened. I did know that it was something bad by the concerned look on the boy's face and the blood on my clothes. I remember seeing cloudy faces of the EMTs emerge and my friend sweating nervously above me. Flash: the sirens making red shadows across the dark roads as we curved to the hospital; flash: asking to use the bathroom in the hospital; flash: dumping the drugs I had on me and insanely thinking: *how can I get more?*

What I was told later and what the police report said was that a call was placed at about 9:30 p.m. on New Year's Eve 1999. A teen boy called to report that his friend was found in the bathroom alone, having a seizure, bleeding from her nose and foaming at the mouth. Her body was convulsing and rigid. The doctor would later say that I almost went into cardiac arrest from a cocaine overdose and could easily have died. Should have died.

When my parents showed up, I knew it was over. I could see it on their disappointed faces from the hospital room doorway. They thought I was better. They thought treatment had cured me. I pretended like it had. Now, there was nowhere to run, nowhere to hide. And laying there in those cold white sheets, my head throbbing and stomach churning, all I could do was think about how I could get the out of there. All I could do was think about how I could escape.

I carried so much pain in my young heart, but I had no idea what to do with it. I had a taste of recovery, but I hadn't found community. I was angry at God, but I didn't know that it was okay to be. Untreated, alone, ashamed—the pain just multiplied. My thorny addictions broke me to the point of despair. The gift of desperation.

In *The Tropic of Cancer*, writer Henry Miller says: "I need to be alone. I need to ponder my shame and my despair in seclusion; I need the sunshine and the paving stones of the streets without companions, without conversation, face to face with myself, with only the music of my heart for company."

He was wrong. What I needed then was light and community and shared experience and understanding. I needed someone to walk alongside me and not only listen, but share their story of hurt and brokenness, too.

Later on, there was a moment when I fell to the floor and looked up and cried: "God, save me!" It wasn't that night in the hospital, but it was coming.

Part 2:
UP FROM THE BASEMENT

Chapter 9:
TESTING THE WATERS

*Then love knew it was called love. And when I lifted my eyes
to your name, suddenly your heart showed me the way.*
– Pablo Neruda

fter I had been going to church for a year or so and trying
(and failing) to stay sober, my friend asked me if I knew
Jesus.

"Who?"

I was a little startled by the question and that was my gut response:
To answer in the form of a question. Of course, I knew him. We sang
about him, read his words in red ink, talked about him; women in
funky hats exclaimed "Praise Jesus!" when the pastor took a breath.
We even ate and drank him (as the eucharist), as *Twilight*-esque as
that seemed to me at the time.

As a kid, I did not have many experiences of church other than
attending an old Methodist church with my grandpa (who turned
off his hearing aids and sat in the last row); and the evangelical youth

group I attended with Chloe before drugs took priority, where we ate pizza and sang songs about not hiding our light under a bushel as I wondered why the adult volunteers weren't drinking beer. I went to places where they talked about Jesus, but I never experienced him. I thought the whole thing was sort of outdated. Irrelevant.

"You know, Jesus," my friend clarified with added emphasis on the "sus" part.

I felt like a character in *Blue Like Jazz*. Perhaps my name could be Caroline the Wanderer. Then I got to thinking: the Jesus I heard about in the New Testament (when I actually listened), the radical who hung out with drunks and sex workers and who told stories about farmers and widows and who healed the lowest of the low like lepers and women and who could heal with just a touch or word, the guy who lived so counterculturally, he shocked the big-wigs of his day?

"No."

I did not know this Jesus.

I remember knowing that there was something out there as a child. Whenever I had to take the trash out, carrying two large bins down a midnight-black driveway, I'd look toward the starry night, the air smelling of campfire, and marvel at the distant twinkling specks like a July night of fireflies flipped on its head and suspended above me. How amazing to live on a gigantic, spinning orb circling a ball of fire in a galaxy that is only one in trillions. It was too much to comprehend and yet I loved to ponder it all. It made me even want to search, to know, what that something out there was. But despite the songs and games and pizza and preaching, I don't remember anyone ever telling me. Despite the fact that I had been going to church for a couple years during undergrad and I was hearing the sermons and singing the songs and of course I loved the worship music—I don't remember anyone ever telling me who He *really* was. Outside of the tradition and formality and stories and felt boards: Who was this Jesus?

Like most borderline millennials and Gen Xer's (I'm still not 100% sure what category I fit into), I was also quite familiar with the notion that lots of churches are judgmental and hypocritical and looked down on people like me, people who had committed innumerable sins, and even (admittedly) had fun doing some of them. In college, I had walked by plenty of "sidewalk prophets" telling me and my friends that we were going to hell. I've even had holy water shot at me from a distance by a water gun. I've rolled my eyes while driving by mega churches that sprawl across city blocks, with parking lots the size of the Pentagon adjacent to communities with low-income housing; and lots of my weed-induced late-night talks with pseudo-friends have included lingering questions about why the church, in some ways, isn't really that distinguishable from the rest of the world. As Gandhi has been famously quoted: "I like your Christ, I do not like your Christians. Your Christians are so unlike your Christ."

But despite my resentment, questions, doubt and jazzy ramblings about the topic, someone finally asked and I answered:

"Yes, I'd like to know this Jesus."

I had an inkling that Jesus was about more than what I had reduced religion to. After I experienced what I had in high school, I was ready to accept just about anything.

My friend came with me to talk to the pastor of the church and it was decided that I was going to be baptized. I say "it was decided" because it felt like it just needed to happen. Like when I just needed to grow out my baby bangs. If I was going to get to know this Jesus, getting baptized seemed like a good place to start. At the time I wasn't sure I bought in to the tradition, but I knew it couldn't hurt. In *Jesus Feminist*, Sarah Bessey says that "this is the mark of a soul in pursuit of Jesus: we recognize him." I didn't know him (I admitted as much), but there was something about his face. Like I knew him from somewhere.

For years (in fact, I just recently donated it), I've kept the dress I wore on my baptism: it was cream colored and flowing with large pink lilies and had a bright pink ribbon that tied at the front—the reason I love lilies to this day. The pastor decided that Easter was a great time to be baptized. It was me and another baby. I was too excited to be humiliated. It was not until years later that I learned in the early church, Easter was *the* day for baptisms. I still remember the picture from that day, my smile and the brightness in my eyes.

Henri Nouwen said that "the Christian [...] believes that God is not "something," but rather a person who is Love – perfect love." This is what I had been searching for, for so long: *Someone* to love me. Of course, my life did not instantly get happy, sober or free the minute I was baptized. But I began a journey, one that led towards more questions. A door opened and I walked through it with my flowing lily dress on.

After this particular Easter, I experienced trauma again. I used drugs and alcohol again, and I hurt myself again and again. In large, open circles, I would hear people talk about a higher power outside of themselves that shook them awake. Something—someone—who was the reason for a complete and total life change. I heard countless stories of being made new, something that I longed to find and experience. Even though I accepted the invitation, it took me some time before I could let this *Someone* love me.

One night I found myself at the bar again. This was a couple years after the lily dress and trying out church. I was trying to stay sober alone and failing miserably, every day promising that I wasn't going to go out or get that bottle or baggie and then doing it anyway.

I stumbled into the dark room after the thought of one more minute alone in my smokey apartment felt intolerable. Though I was terrified of being around other people, especially men, if I had enough alcohol or pot, I could forget about that for a little while. It was on one such evening that I can see pieces thrown in front of me:

Purple haze in a dark, crowded room. My head moves back and forth with the music, sweat beads at the back of my neck. It feels good to be so uninhibited. To not care what I look like or what people think. I am surrounded by people on all sides—in fact I can feel some of them brushing up against me; strange hands touching the small of my back as they pass to make it back to the bar for another drink or to the bathroom that smells like Walmart cologne and toilet water. Light caresses on my arm when they try to start a conversation.

There is so much movement and life, and for a moment I am confident. Bold. I feel empowered as I take up my private space on the dance floor. For a brief instant, like I am fourteen again and holding my arms in the air as Chloe and I float across the cornfields with our strawberry wine. Music swirls. Hips grace side-to-side. Eyes closed. Eyes open. Eyes closed again. Then I turn and see him dancing nearby with a friend. We went on a couple dates back in high school. He drove a fast car and had California blonde hair. Hair is still blonde. I think to myself: I'll call you *California*. Car probably still fast. The music, all of a sudden, sounds louder. He comes closer. Smile. Hello. He leans in.

I don't want a hug.

His mouth smells like a Bud Light commercial.

He keeps talking and I'm not listening, only looking around for my friends.

Did I come here by myself?

I can't remember.

Either way, now I'm alone in the crowd and want to leave.

What I remember next: driving home drunk, staring at the center lines, trying to stay inside them. The sky seems blacker than usual.

Where are the stars tonight? Pulling in to the parking lot, inching towards my spot in the back corner right under the flickering street light. It glows gold onto the pavement as I get out, shut the door (did I lock it?), checking again and then making my way, holding a key between two fingers like my daddy taught me. Looking behind me all the way to my front door.

I open the door. My cat jumps from her spot on the armrest of the green sofa and meets me as I struggle to get the black boots off and throw keys onto the table. I close the door with my foot and then exhale as I lock the deadbolt, then lock the chain link above it. So many locks to keep a single woman safe. I check and recheck to make sure it's locked. In the kitchen, which is basically the dining room as it's the smallest version of a one-bedroom apartment I could afford in the city, pouring a glass of water. It feels cool in my mouth, traveling down my throat, my body craving hydration.

Then—knock. Knock. Knock.

I startle when I hear the soft tapping on the door. It gets louder.

Knock, knock, knock.

Then the pounding.

My cat gets up from her warm indent on the sofa, where she returned to once I closed the door, and runs away. I'm worried my neighbors are going to call the police.

Knock, knock, knock.

Never think about calling the police myself.

I open the door a crack.

Tell him to leave.

He pushes the door into me and stumbles in.

I ask him to leave again.

He's saying something—I'm not sure what.

"Leave. Please, leave." I try to yell, but I can't hear myself anymore.

Am I talking?

I wake up half-dressed with my head pounding and crawl to the bathroom. He is gone. When did he leave? I try to recollect but all I can envision… then gagging, hanging my head over the cold toilet. I stare into the clear water; glad I had just cleaned it. Wondering if I should get one of those blue things that you put in the bowl and it keeps it dark cobalt blue like at cheap chain restaurants. After a few moments, I start the shower. The hot water falls onto my skin and I stand there for a long time letting it.

In the Bible, there are two words used for time: "Chronos" and "Kairos." Chronos refers to time like we generally think of it: hours in a day, chronological or sequential time. Kairos is something else entirely. In the ancient Greek it means the "right, critical or opportune moment."[27] There are numerous mentions of Kairos in scripture and this ancient word, according to Bible scholars, has a more nuanced meaning than just the right and opportune moment.[28] Kairos "calls for action, conversion and transformation— [...] a moment of grace."[29]

Right before Jesus began his ministry, he was baptized by John and then spent forty days being tempted by Satan in the desert. He hung out with wild animals. He chilled with angels. He refuted and rebuffed Satan's crafty ways of trying to trick him or tempt him away from his divine purpose. Just writing this sentence is exhausting. Jesus was busy in the desert. And hungry. Not only was he brought to the brink, he fasted for 40 days and nights not having a single crust of moldy bread. He felt what it means to be fully human and then some.

Immediately after these trials and period of testing, Jesus went into Galilee to preach the good news. At this exact moment, John was imprisoned because of his ministry of baptism. The pieces had fallen in to place. God flung the doors of Kairos open.

Jesus said:

> The time [Kairos] has come. The kingdom of God has
> come near. Repent and believe the good news.[30]

There was so much that hung in the balance for Jesus, for just the right time to begin his work in the world. He experienced his season of temptation just like any other human being on earth. He escaped the victor and did it without sin, unlike anyone. God brought him through those fiery, hunger-laden moments, before he was to begin his ministry on Earth. In scripture as in life, chronological time crashes into that perfect opportunity or moment that God creates in our lives for His good purposes.

This can all be tough to wade through when what lurks in the murky waters is trauma and angst and addiction.

John Piper says that "love has to do with showing a dying soul the life-giving beauty of the glory of God, especially his grace."[31] This grace, the beautiful and mysterious thing, started inching its way in. But only after the death and despair. After being baptized and making a decision to continue to seek the something or someone I knew I was missing, things didn't get better. But they got clearer. I realized that God's wacked out love was for me, too. Even if I was raped again.

Chapter 10:

NO LASER LIGHT SHOWS, PLEASE

When life throws you a bag of sorrow, hold out your hands.
— Kate Baer

In *Having a Mary Heart in a Martha World*, Joanna Weaver says that she felt profound relief when she got to the point of realizing that "Christianity is a process and not an event. It is a journey and not a destination."[32] Intimacy with God is something that is born out of a relationship. And for many (like me), born out of struggle. It was when I moved to Michigan after college (long story for another day) that my relationship with God started getting serious. We went from texting occasionally to swiping right and actually meeting face to face for coffee. But it was still complicated.

I met a woman right out of college that had some interesting perspectives on the church. When I met Nora, I had put the drugs and alcohol down and I felt my relationship with God and connection to something greater than me growing, but my pain hadn't evaporated and my life was still teetering (depending on the day) on insanity. I wish it worked that way—instant healing. I've always been a fan of instant gratification. When I want something, I want it now (thanks, Amazon).

Nora wasn't someone who hadn't tried it. As she said she "dabbled in faith like pot." Nor did she consider herself an atheist. She said she was more of an agnostic Christian. Someone who believed in Jesus and all the rest, even wanted to follow him, but because of what she saw in the church, wasn't sure she wanted to associate with religion anymore. Wasn't sure about any of it. She affectionately called herself an "ex-vangelical" though she admitted that she didn't think she was really ever an evangelical either.

"Aren't they all Republicans?" she said one day in more of a statement than question.

Nora told me about the time she tried church when she was getting sober. The building was within walking distance from her recovery home. She and a couple of the other ladies hung around the back door having cigarettes and drinking coffee from stained secondhand mugs. As they stood there in frayed jean jackets and parachute pants (I swear it's not 1985) waiting for the service to start so they could go in late, watching the Sunday traffic and the men approaching in suit jackets and overcoats and the women in heels, they couldn't help but notice the way people looked at them. Or more accurately, didn't look at them. Nora explained:

"They looked at us by not looking at us. That is, they looked quick, then away. Or, I guess you could say that it felt like they looked right through us. The only other time I felt like that was when I was homeless for a couple months and the women walked by with their hundred-dollar shoes and leather bags and click, click, click, right on by."

It didn't get any better when they went in, either, she said. They could tell right away that people were avoiding them.

"I think we made things uncomfortable…and for the American church," she laughed, "this is close to heresy."

Eventually, the women from the sober home, including Nora, decided to spend more time outside the sanctuary, standing under the awning, even in the rain. It was easier. Sometimes the music of the worship band made it outside or shadows of the blue strobe lights flashing reached them and they nodded along. But most times, they hung there inhaling and exhaling sweet smelling vape or cigarette smoke and talking. Outside, they could avoid the avoidance.

I understood Nora's experience.

Church and I have always had a complicated relationship, too. People I knew who called themselves Christians, the self-proclaimed "devout" or "religious" types, were some of the most messed up people I knew. I had also heard the news over the years, like everyone who can afford a smart phone, about those ordained or *chosen* who did horrible things to children like the Catholic priests overseas and those closer to home. I've also seen with my own eyes believers who spent long days in the cold and rain holding signs that spew hate, not love, towards others.

Church, to me at the time, seemed to contradict itself, at once proclaiming the good news of love and peace and healing and also acting out the basest of human tendencies: pride and hate. Or it focused on all the wrong things. Not kingdom stuff. False eye lashes for sermons. Starbuck's in the lobby. Everyone looking like a "this is a paid ad" influencer. What Rachel Held Evans dissects so eloquently in *Searching for Sundays*.[33] If you live in a world saturated by addiction and sexual trauma, as I did, how will having a laser lightshow at your service really help bring Jesus closer?

Nora made me laugh when she'd go on about pastors with thick black-rimmed glasses or Portland accents or churches that have parking ramps and their own social media consultants. She grinned mischievously when she told me everyone was trying too hard to be "relevant." To be in and of the world. Nora said they just ended up looking ridiculous. Or like statues, like the ones her grandmother used to paint around Christmas time. Giant Marys and Josephs and Wise Men who are stagnant, immovable. Quiet. But with excellent contour make-up and background lighting.

Nora explained how those basement meetings with the tired, joy-filled people smoking outside is the church where she felt most comfortable. It was alive. Breathing. Bleeding. Real. The Sunday, dress-up, sing sweet and nod quietly—these churches were never for her.

One afternoon, I met Nora for coffee and we strolled up and down the main street of the city and watched as the buildings around us grew, kissing the sky. Some were old construction from a hundred years ago, antique blocks and marble. Some were being built with cranes and orange fencing, open concept, all bones and four-by-fours. She was moving out of the sober living home and I asked if she was worried about going back out there. The transition from addiction treatment can be a scary time; the opportune moment for a setback.

"No, I'm not worried. Relapse doesn't even feel like an option anymore."

I was happy for her. I knew her story, the in and out of treatment, the back and forth, the near brushes with death that kept her tethered to the grim reality of addiction. Her own version of sexual violence and mental health challenges. And I knew her experience, because I had lived it, too. I also knew that hope, despite the struggle of the past and the weight of shame, was out there waiting.

She told me she was still going to meetings, still going to church. "If it works, work it—that's what my sponsor says."

Despite my own reservations about church (and shall I dare say judgements?), a couple years after meeting Nora, I joined a small group of women around my age who were deemed to be in the "transitional stage" of life. In church-ese, I learned that this is the stage after college when women are "young professionals" and cool aunts: women who had outgrown the church youth group but are too young for the adult Bible studies (i.e., would find them "lame"). Women who are still single or going on respectable dates (dates with lots of slobbery kissing and fantasizing about going further and then praying on shaky knees for God to forgive their lusty ways and help them to be "in the world but not of it").

I joined this group of women around my age and was terrified because they seemed annoyingly wholesome. It was my first experience with a group of upstairs church ladies. They were women who I thought were nothing at all like me and couldn't understand my experience in the least. For someone who longed to belong and worshiped the idea of inclusion, I wanted nothing to do with them.

We met at the leader of the group's house, a woman named Lisa. She was one of the "cool aunt" types and a young professional who had a brand-new condo that looked like it was the complex's staged unit. Everything was immaculate and fashionably up-to-date for the time, decorated in shades of burgundy, brown and navy. She offered us tea, which seemed odd to me (no one my age had ever offered me tea). One of the other women was a singer in the worship band and a teacher who looked edgy and fun in that Christian rock band kind of way. Another was a bit more relatable, had a young daughter (out of wedlock) and wore her pain so everyone could see it. There were other women, too, who lived life and struggled with things like over-eating, misery in singleness, depression, and anxiety.

I started to look up to them in a way, women who I was learning might not be *that different* than me, but who were able to show up and not be so fricking terrified and uncomfortable just to be sitting on a floor, holding someone else's sofa pillow and drinking hot tea out of a pretty mug. Showing up on Monday nights for me was like being a contestant on *American Ninja Warrior*. I had to battle everything in my mind that popped up and told me that I didn't belong and never would. I scaled a wall of sorts, the seemingly unscalable, just to open the front door and give everyone the customary half-smile and say "Hello, how are you?"

Slowly, week after week, I'd maniacally chew my Nicorette gum from work to Lisa's (by that time, I'd quit smoking) and take deep breaths in and out until I shut my door and reminded myself to take out my Nicorette or I might pass out while we said the opening prayer. We studied books like *What Do You Do with Your Wait* and talked about what it was like to be in such a time of our life. I went along with it (though I didn't feel like I was waiting for anything) and read the scripture passages but rarely spoke and when I did, had to push out every word with force. For me, this wasn't a transitional period—this was it. I'd been given a life preserver and was floating, completely content in some ways. God saved me when I was sinking and now, as far as I was concerned, this is all there had to be and that was more than enough.

Yet the anxiety over sharing my life, being vulnerable or real with others—women or men—made me want to vomit. Occasionally (very occasionally) I'd get the courage to go out to dinner or for a walk on the boardwalk or have someone from the church group over for lunch. I didn't realize it until much later how deep my little scars really were. As they say in recovery circles, I white-knuckled it and hung on tight, trying to heal in the illusion of my safe, solitary closet, just like the one I used to hide in as a kid at my grandpa's house. But despite the fear, I mustered the strength to carry on with it. Despite my own doubts and feeling out of place and too broken, I knew there was something mysterious and healing about being with other people.

One Sunday morning, I drove to church and came to a familiar bend in the road. It's one of my favorite spots (and still is), because as you approach the almost ninety-degree right turn, it feels as if you are about to drive right into the clouds. Every Sunday, I always slowed almost to a stop as I approached, even when someone was behind me, so that I could get a good look of the view that opened up as I'd get closer: the town's main beach and expanse of blue water that reaches into the horizon with its majestic hands.

When I arrived, I got out of my car slowly, making sure to not have to talk to anyone. For me, going to church, the physical act of going, required prayer. Walking in, not wanting to be noticed, trying to find a seat that's not too close to the front but not the last row, either. Making sure I have enough of my own bubble to not have a panic attack. Let me tell you, for women like me, it can be exhausting just figuring out where to sit in a crowd that feels safe. Sometimes I had anxiety attacks that came out of nowhere (I have a name for them now), leaving my heart racing and hands sweaty cold.

The service began like it usually did and I felt a bit more comfortable as the lights dimmed and the crowd around me disappeared. On this particular Sunday, I wasn't sure if it was the drive or the music or the way the light hit the water, but I felt a bit calmer than usual and a bit more comfortable. The first couple songs ended, the announcements were made, and then the pastor—a middle-aged man with graying hair who liked to wear blue jeans (thankfully, not of the skinny variety)—began to speak.

He started with a laugh and then a story, as most pastors do. The story began with a woman who had been sexually abused. I thought: "Wait...did I hear this right?"

I didn't feel ready for this.

The pastor went on with his navy-blue eyes. I didn't hear all of what he said; I'd graze in and out of the hearing, but he talked about the pain and the betrayal she felt, how she always questioned the existence of God because *how could a loving God exist if this happened to her?*

Yes, I was hearing this right.

It felt like the story was directed right to me.

"God was there," he said, "the whole time. He was standing in the door way, by the side of the bed. He was holding your hand through it all. Jesus wept."

He looked up and I swear made eye contact with me, at least that's how it felt. Sort of like when you at a concert and think the lead singer is looking at you (by the way, everyone thinks this). I knew that God was speaking through this story on this particular Sunday to reach a particular place inside of me that was still hiding in a dark corner.

On the bathroom floor.

And again—with the heavy door pushing into me.

Falling down.

The tears rolled in heavy waves down my cheeks and my chest heaved. I don't know how the people around me perceived what was happening because at that moment there was only one other person in the room. That was the day I believed with my whole heart.

God was there when it happened—when all of it happened.

He lay down beside me in the snow bank and held my hand as I laid on the bathroom floor.

He wept when my apartment door was pushed in and I disappeared again.

God did not will these things to happen to me.

We live in a broken world.

I was the collateral damage. Though, to Him, I was not damaged at all and never was. To him, I was and have always been and will always be His beloved.

Beautiful, beloved.

God was there.

Encounter. Not dry theology or half-baked ideas. No judgements or artificial smiles. None of the niceties. None of the lies. Something happened in that church service that I couldn't explain. Something spiritual.

Something I didn't know still happened in church buildings.

Dr. Katie McCoy, the director of women's ministry at Baptist General Convention of Texas, wrote an article on how sexual assault is portrayed in the Bible, titled *God is not silent*. She notes how the "Lord takes up the cause of the victim and the vulnerable. Deuteronomy 22:25-27 safeguarded the survivor of sexual assault from being unjustly blamed or ignored."[34] Importantly, there are also two accounts of sexual assault mentioned after this passage: the "Unnamed Concubine" in Judges 19 and Tamar in 2 Samuel 13. Dr. McCoy also notes how the word "chazaq" is used to describe these scenes, which in Hebrew implies violence.[35] While it might have been culturally acceptable for some, these actions were seen in God's eyes as one of the vilest and most violent of acts.

God's love and law surrounded women in the past and is living and active today. The world might be a broken place, but God is still just and loving and can feel our struggle and humanity in the very core of who He is. God upholds the struggle of women—and men—alike.

At this church service, this was comforting to me in a way that I had never experienced before. The sermon I heard that Sunday morning was exactly what I needed to hear, exactly when I needed to hear it. And interestingly, after this, my view of church started to shift, too. If I was loved and held and cared for, despite my own brokenness and broken past experiences, others were, too. I did not have to let my resentment or bitterness choke out what was trying to grow around me in those walls that had once felt so suffocating and unsafe. It was okay to start letting people know me. It is okay to be known.

Chapter 11:
SWEET BALM
FOR A BROKEN SOUL

No one is more aware of the passage of time than a convert.
There is a clear before and after whose threshold
is a life-changing encounter with Christ.[36]
– Rev. John Henry Hanson

O ne of the many things I love about recovery is that for many, helping others is about sharing our experience, strength and hope. It's not advice. It's not condescension or lecturing. It's about understanding. Listening. Being genuine. Telling our stories. No sugar-coating or sound bite versions. No TikTok or Reels or tweets. The truth. "Nothing is such balm for a broken soul as this—to know you are not alone."[37]

Alex was one young woman who allowed me the honor of listening to her share her life. I met her at an outpatient behavioral health clinic called Connections Counseling, where I started mentoring young people in recovery after I moved back home from Michigan. I was still going to church, or church-hopping (like I used to bar-hop), but still having trouble connecting. Even though I didn't wear my shame-stained coat anymore, it was still there, all stank, in a heap on the backseat.

I met an older woman at my newest church who encouraged me to get involved with a recovery community.

"Doesn't this go against Christianity?" I asked her, sort of appalled she thought that I was missing something. I was in my twenties and thought I knew everything—or if I didn't, at least I could look it up on the internet.

"I have a friend who has been going to meetings for years and gets a lot out of them. Connection. Community."

I was at a breaking point again (I'll get to that in a minute, his name was Beau) and decided to give it a try. After attending a couple different recovery meetings, I ended up going to outpatient groups and volunteering my time to work with other women in recovery. They said being of service would help me stay outside of my head and stay sober. So, like getting baptized, I gave it a try.

This behavioral health clinic is where I met Tanya, my best friend Ell, and so many other young people in addiction and mental health recovery.

Despite her own traumas, over time Alex began opening her heart to me. She told me about her parent's marriage, the way some of her family members drank to excess, and how she was jealous of her sister. She asked me questions that I could not answer, like how was wine so different from heroin? She shared her excitement that bubbled up now that she was sober, her disbelief that she would finally be able to study abroad before she got her undergraduate degree in criminal justice. She couldn't wait to help other people not as privileged as her, people who didn't grow up in the suburbs, people caught up in a system of punishment and isolation and addiction that they could not escape.

Alex had questions about God, too.

She grew up going to church with her family, but couldn't reconcile the God she learned about with the way she saw the world. She asked me about my faith in her gentle way. A part of me had to laugh when she asked me these questions. Why was she asking me? Why did she think I had anything at all to say about God and faith? If she only knew me at fifteen when I was snorting cocaine between classes in a bathroom stall. Hanging out with dealers in low-light parking lots, hoping the cops wouldn't show up as the other car pulled away slowly with its lights off. Stumbling from the bar and getting behind the wheel and never getting caught. Didn't she know how my life was one of those afterschool specials they made us watch in elementary school in the early 1990s that did absolutely no good (at least for me)? Who was I to show her the truth behind the little silver cross I wore and the gritty, real-life reasons I wore it?

I wasn't the only person who lived through trauma, used substances to cope with the aftermath and questioned a god that could stand by as the shrapnel fell. Alex, in her own quiet way, helped me to see that I was not alone in my experience—or my doubts. God was there with me through it all, as I had felt so completely during that church service before I started my journey into recovery with community. And I could share that experience with her.

Until I got the call and shut myself in the bathroom and sobbed. In my mind's eye, I saw her red hair and devastatingly beautiful eyes. Tiny details circled in my mind: her chipped green nail polish, the way her lips moved around her lip ring when she spoke; her raspy voice; her obsession with all things Harry Potter; her black lace-up boots. The way she walked with her gaze down. I knew she was hiding things. She hid her eyes from the world because she didn't want anyone to see her. To *really* see her. I knew she was hiding because I recognized myself in her. *Me, too*, we whispered back and forth without words as I drove her to recovery meetings and we talked and smoked cigarettes and she'd ask me what recovery was like and I would tell her, usually without words, that it was amazing.

Alex was twenty-three years old when she died from a heroin overdose in her childhood bedroom. Her mother found her in the morning. Her body was draped across the floor, half in her open closet. Next to her was a red plaid slipper and a needle.

I was in shock. I kept repeating to myself and to anyone who would listen: *such a waste*. SUCH A WASTE! NO! I wanted to scream loud enough for the world to hear. For all of the people struggling with addiction and their family members and the police officers taking them to jail instead of treatment and the parole officers and the social workers and the women she was supposed to help with her criminal justice degree and to the women like her and like me and maybe like you who have lived through things we shouldn't have.

Such a waste of precious life and possibility and hope.

Since Alex died, I have been to more funerals that I can count for people killed by addiction. I got a special conservative black dress for the occasions. My funeral dress. My addiction funeral dress. If it wasn't someone I knew well, I saw the obituary posted on Facebook or IG first, scroll through the comments of shock, horror, then check their page to make sure. I always go to the last thing they posted before they died and think to myself how haunting this last post must be for family and friends. Sometimes it is sadly a premonition or sometimes it is some random meme or video. If it was someone I knew well, I'd get that call that starts with muffled tears and the three words that preface what I instantly wish I could un-hear: "Have you heard?"

I hate saying that someone has "lost their lives to" addiction. It sounds too passive—like they just succumbed and couldn't find it—

their life—anymore. I don't like to say this because it's not what happens. Addiction steals lives. It thrives on the blood of the innocent and struggling. Addiction devours and destroys families and homes. Addiction leaves an empty seat at the table. Addiction takes away so much from so many. It is more than heartbreaking. Words fall short and break against the pavement like the glass beer bottles I used to throw at stop signs on country roads. If you ask a mother or father who has lost a child to addiction, rarely will they say "they lost their life to addiction." More times than not, there is nothing but gaping sadness and a hollow disbelief if you have courage and compassion to ask what happened.

After Alex's death, once the grief ebbed like the tide inching back to sea, something new started to grow inside me. And it was not death, but anew life: a desire to live for her and for women like her. Alex reminded me of my own brush with death years before, how it could have and should have been me. Why did I live through it when she died because of addiction and the darkness that surrounds it?

"Why do bad things happen? Why does God allow it?"

On one bright summer afternoon, after a two-day drug binge, my boyfriend at the time and I were driving around. I only had strength for the slow inhale of menthol cigarettes and staring out the window. I was nauseous, with every muscle screaming, and my head pulsated with sharp stabs of pain. My nose was raw and red. My baggy flannel was stained from nose bleeds.

After realizing we weren't going to get any more drugs, I held back as long as I could and then watched in the passenger mirror as tears and cigarette smoke mixed with snot. I remember looking into the clouds, cursing the sun that mocked me with its beauty. *How can there be a God,* I remember thinking, *when I feel like this?*

When I was sixteen years old, I spent most of my time getting high. Trying anything to bring my body back to equilibrium. It stopped being "fun" and turned into need. I needed to use in order to feel normal. What I didn't know at that time was that my entire system was regularly flushed with cortisol because of the trauma I'd experienced. I was anxious and fearful and the only coping strategy I had found that worked or tried was self-medicating. Using alcohol and other drugs was a way to run from pain. It worked for a time.

We pulled up to a stop light and I looked to my right. A family stopped next to us in a minivan. The woman was laughing. I saw the outline of car seats in the back, with bobbling legs kicking and small, blonde heads dancing. I could faintly hear singing. All at once, I got angry. My cheeks flushed red and I turned my attention towards God:

"If you are really here, I wouldn't feel like this!"

No answer.

"I could stop."

We pulled away from the red light and I followed the silver minivan as it sped ahead. I imagined the family getting to their destination, a pristine house in the suburbs. I continued my interrogation:

"If you are real, why am I in so much pain?"

Silence.

"God?!?"

Nothing.

Ten years later, when I was a couple years into my addiction recovery, I discovered Philip Yancey in a small library. I was surprised when I read that being a Christian doesn't make my world smaller. In fact, the way of Jesus brings more, not less, to life. He showed me that doubting faith, asking questions, and even struggling with God is all a part of the process. Grace is amazing.

In one of his books, *Disappointment with God*, Philip Yancey asks what my sixteen-year-old-self grappled with during excruciating years of drug use, sexual violence and addiction: "If God has the ability to act fairly, speak audibly, and appear visibly, why, then, does he seem so reluctant to intervene today?"[38]

If God is so good, then why is the world hurting so much? Why do I hurt so much?

Phillip Yancy grew up in the turbulent 1960s, plagued by his own questions and struggle to make sense of the world he lived in. His family, with all of its faithful dysfunction and spiritual trauma, rocked his own sense of stability. He longed to transcend a "toxic faith" and experience something truer: a real relationship with God. For someone like me, who was angry with God but longing for a real connection, Yancey's vocal struggle was like sweet, springtime air. Finally, a Christian who told the truth.

When Yancy was writing his best-selling book, *Where is God When it Hurts?*, and addressing his own stumbling blocks to faith, he discovered a doctor who helped him uncover some life and faith-changing things about pain. Dr. Paul Brand was a child of missionary parents, and he later moved back to India to teach after finishing medical school in the late 1940s. He was challenged by a colleague to use his orthopedic skills to help address some of the horrific results of leprosy: the deforming of the hands and feet. At that time, little was known about this mysterious disease that had such biblical and stigmatizing roots. According to the International Leprosy Association, "it was generally believed that the hands and feet of infected people simply disintegrated or rotted away as a direct result of the disease."[39]

Dr. Brand was one of the leading voices (if not the only voice) championing research for people, including children, with leprosy. Not surprisingly, he faced much resistance to his work as people with leprosy were often shunned by their families and society. Dr. Brand, using what he learned working with veterans and polio patients, came up with a new theory. He discovered that the deformities weren't caused by the disease itself but by infections. Leprosy is disease of the nervous system. When his patients didn't feel pain, that is when injuries happened. What was wrong wasn't treated because it could not be felt.

In many of his books, Yancey talks in depth about his interviews with Dr. Brand and what he learned from him. They even co-wrote a few books together. Dr. Brand and his research had a profound impact on Yancey and in an unexpected way opened up a new door (or perhaps an old door in a new way, theologically speaking): pain has a purpose.

In *Soul Survivor*, Yancey writes of Brand: "He invited me to consider an alternative world without pain. He insisted on pain's great value, holding up as proof the terrible results of leprosy—damaged faces, blindness, and loss of fingers, toes, and limbs—all of which occur as side-effects of painlessness."[40]

Dr. Brand helped Yancey understand the value of pain in a new way. "The purpose of pain, it's like a language. It's your body's most effective language to get you to pay attention to a wound."[41] Even through the pain, or perhaps because of it, redemption and healing is possible.

While pain and trauma can have detrimental and deadly effects in our lives, God can and does transform our experience. Dr. Brand learned this. Philip Yancey learned this. And I, a woman in addiction and trauma recovery, am learning this, too.

After his own beatings, imprisonments, persecutions, and other sufferings, the Apostle Paul wrote:

And we know that in all things God works for the good of those who love him, who have been called according to his purpose.[42]

A verse like this might give you the heart-tingles, but for other folks, for me at different points in my life, it has churned me into an angry psalmist who's shaking cold fists into the air. Or like a disgruntled boxer—maybe Mike Tyson right before he bit someone's ear lobe off. Over time, however, I have been able to look back at those events in my life: the trauma, sexual violence, addiction and loss, with grace—even acceptance. Even if we do have to look up at the shining sun in anguish, with questions, with doubt, with anger, God hears even when he is silent.

A lot of people think it says if you love God only good things will happen to you. It doesn't say that at all. It says that God can use even the worst things you experience. You can never be separated from God's Love. God will find a way.[43]

Or put another way by Yancey: God is the great recycler. He can turn or redeem or make beautiful even the most tragic experiences. Even if you might not yet believe it or have trouble reading the words, know that you are not alone. Struggle might be a part of the story, but it's not the only chapter. With doubt can come a new faithful beginning. With pain and hurt, redemption.

After Alex died, I tried to pray but didn't hear a sound and this made me even more confused. I tried to talk about it in small group at church, but the women (it seemed) just looked on with pity. They lacked understanding. Empathy. Was it stigma that prevented any true heart connection? Was it overwhelm? Is there too much pain in the world to be able to keep our hearts open to all of it? Where was God's thunderous voice through soft eyes?

Despite my questions and doubts, I told God that regardless of the fact that I didn't understand any of it, I was going to show up. I didn't know why women like Alex had to die when women like me made it out alive, but because it was the way it was, I decided I was going to do something with my life. Alex's short life birthed a desire in my heart to sacrifice everything I had ever known since I began my recovery journey, everything I thought I would ever do, everything that once brought me joy, to provide a place for her or women like her (and like me) a shelter from the storm—or better, a shelter in one.

After you've been in recovery for a little while, and God knocks you off your horse or shatters you with grief or shows up through the love of others, you start to think that anything is possible. You begin to believe that those dreams you had when you were a kid weren't so silly after all. Or maybe on your way to finding a dream you realize you are chasing the wrong one. Alex dying was another encounter, a conversion, an opening. A friend in recovery told me once that grief opens the heart. When someone dies, the place in your heart where they once lived empties and widens and something new is given room to grow in its emptiness.

Chapter 12:
FLUTTER BY BUTTERFLIES

*Lying there, Ma said, "You all listen now, this is a real lesson in
life. Yes, we got stuck, but what'd we girls do? We made it fun,
we laughed. That's what sisters and girlfriends are all about.
Sticking together even in the mud, 'specially in mud."*
– Delia Owen, Where the Crawdads Sing

The first time I left inpatient treatment as a teen, I returned
home to the same environment that I left. The same friends
and problems met me when I returned. I felt like a changed
person, with resolve and ready to begin life again, ready to be healthy
and choose well and treat my body with respect. But it was not until I
was able to change everything about my surroundings, including who
I was surrounding myself with, that I was able to build something new
on a strong foundation.

Don Coyhis of the Native American *Wellbriety* recovery movement talks about the metaphor of the healing forest. A summary of
the metaphor is as follows:

We dig it up, we plant it temporarily in rich soil and fertilizers, we provide it ample sunshine and water. We give it love and attention [...]. The tree doesn't just survive; it thrives in the new conditions. It grows tall and strong; its leaves return green and full. The time comes to place the tree back in its forest and though it stays strong for some time it eventually falls ill again, for after all, the entire forest is malnourished. It is not just the other nearby trees in the forest that effect [*sic*] our tree's well-being, it is also the soil that influences the entire forest's well-being. They are all intertwined down to their root systems and we see that we cannot heal the tree individually, for the root systems are affected by seen and unseen factors.[44]

Recovery is about so much more than quitting drugs and alcohol. According to Coyhis, it is imperative that a "healing forest" is created for the person returning, the one who wants with every cell of their being to live a new, transformed life. I did not know about the research or the science at the time God placed the little dream in my heart to start a recovery home called Connect House. All I knew was this idea I could not shake and the feeling that little by little I was being equipped for a work that I was far from qualified for.

Lori Criss, the associate director of the Ohio Council of Behavioral Health & Family Services Providers says that recovery homes provide people in recovery "with the opportunity to continually surround themselves with other people who are pursuing the same goal of recovery and wellness. It's a place where people can fit in, have common experiences and goals, and can be authentic without having to explain their addiction or recovery needs."[45] They are about accountability and love, offering a place to daily confess shortcomings and celebrate growth—recovery homes are those places with new soil and sunlight, places not just to live but to live in community and genuine fellowship with others. Recovery homes are like the early church in scripture, the early church in the book of Acts, where sharing meals, sharing hearts, and sharing struggle happens. Out loud.

Now for my scientist hat: Data is important. People who are given opportunities to live in recovery housing have better success rates in maintaining long-term recovery than those who do not.[46,47] There is also evidence that suggests there are other incredible outcomes like reduced probability of recurrence of use,[48] lower rates of incarceration,[49] increased employment and income in the future,[50] and improved family relationships and functioning.[51]

I saw this firsthand through the many women who came in and out of the doors of Connect House. Women who showed up beaten down, carrying a small, worn knapsack of their belongings, and a sad but curious look. Women leaving with jobs and school degrees and healed family relationships. The list (and miracles) goes on. For some, these blessings might not have happened right away but they were out there—opportunities like stars hovering.

One of the important lessons I learned in starting a recovery home is how my own healing is connected with working with others. One of the foundational principles of recovery and what is talked about (for some of us, ad nauseum) in the downstairs church: being of service.

Madeline was one of the first women to move into the home, and she had lived a more than eccentric life. She had been an artist and lived on the streets of shiny New York until a lifestyle of heavy drinking and other activities lifestyle brought her from a six-figure income to begging for tossed coins in the subway. Madeline was tough with thick, golden hair that fell past her waist in long braids that swung as she walked. Each of her fingers were etched with handmade tattoos: a star, a cross and a peace sign, all made with black, shaky ink. Madeline's family were either dead or weren't present (ever) the way she needed them to be, so she never approached any of us staff or other residents until she felt safe enough to do so. This took a while.

Madeline, along with being amazingly artistic—she could sew or paint or cook or do pretty much anything creatively, including looking stylish on a zero-dollar clothing budget—was an incredible gardener. She spent long fall afternoons clearing gardens and prepping her little seedling pots and all the things that plant people do to get ready for winter. Winter was a slow, somewhat depressing time. A lot of television and card games and sewing patches on old jeans and walking the couple blocks to a bakery that let some of the residents hang out whenever. Then in spring, Madeline got a giddy skip in her step and was planting seeds and building green bean trellises, and I was driving her to local greenhouses to check out things she would eventually save up money to buy with earnings from her new job.

One of my favorite things to do was listen to Madeline tell stories. She was also one of those people that, although she kept you at a distance, talked and talked—a lot; almost as if she was just waiting for you to interrupt her and say "that's enough" and she could walk away and think to herself dejectedly, "told you so." But I stuck around and listened and learned and took in all of her past lives and future hopes as if they were my own.

Like most women—most people—in recovery, we can easily see our own reflection in someone else's experience. The pain that we all share is not that far apart, even if the specifics of that pain are. And just like people in my past had reflected what I needed to see back to me, I tried to do the same with the women I met, women like Madeline. It was my way of handing her a little circular mirror where she could see herself and see herself beloved.

One afternoon, I stopped by to pick up rent checks and check on the cleaning schedule (all the ladies had to rotate chores, which was sometimes a problem for the women who, like I, hated cleaning someone else's toilet). Madeline was in the kitchen arranging her succulent plants by the window. Everything needed to be just so. One thing I could definitely relate to was her need for things to be organized, to appear controlled, around her.

"Hey."

"Hey," she chimed back and I nodded and went to check out what I needed to check out (there was a lot more business involved in running a nonprofit than I realized). "How are you, Madeline? The plants look amazing as usual."

"Happy, green little friends," she said and smiled.

I could tell she was watching my every move as I checked this and that.

Looking into the basket where all the ladies put rent checks for the month, I noticed that one was missing. I shuffled through them again to make sure I wasn't missing something.

"It's not in there," Madeline explained.

It wasn't her check; she had a distant relative pay until she was able to herself and she was one of the most consistent with the rent and any of the chores or other responsibilities. Sober Madeline was dutiful and purposeful and made sure to check things off the list because she had learned, like I had, how amazing it was to be able to do the normal, adult, grown-up things. What a gift it was to make a grocery list, make a bed, make a friend.

One of the other residents was late with rent again and I didn't know what to do. Madeline instinctively knew that I was struggling with this because I had alluded to as much the month before, how money was tight, how it was so tough to run a small nonprofit with only volunteer help and having to fundraise and do all of those things while all the board members and other volunteers were straining to keep things afloat. I didn't have to say anything, but she knew after she had asked how Connect House was doing financially and I just smiled and changed the subject.

While recovery homes are extremely important and part of an evidence-based approach to helping women maintain successful recoveries, many are underfunded or nonexistent because it takes a lot of work and a steady stream of income, and buffer income, for those who are unable to pay or set up scholarships, which is what we did. The last thing we wanted to do was kick someone out because they couldn't pay. Instead, we raised funds and sought community support. Sometimes our own board members paid the rent of residents who were unable to because of credit debt, school loans, losing their minimum wage jobs or not being able to work when working through significant trauma. Other times, residents couldn't get jobs because of what they had to put under the question "Have you ever been convicted of a crime?" at the bottom of job applications. There wasn't a box that asked if a traumatic history led you into a life you didn't recognize or a box that asked if you were trying to live a transformed life, but needed help to get there.

Madeline, being a bit older than the other women, soon became a mother-figure for many of the ladies. This was particularly interesting, she told me one evening as a group of us sat on the porch listening to city crickets and the purr of traffic a couple blocks down, because she never really had a mom. Not in the traditional sense, anyway. Madeline went on to become the house mentor, someone who more formally mentored the ladies and checked in with staff and got free room and board in exchange. It was amazing to see her grow and blossom like one of her seedlings: first so fragile, then as her roots developed and sunk heartily into the soil, she drank up all the water she could, soaked in all the sun that spilled from the sky to where she was planted, and finally bloomed into the most beautiful flower you have ever seen, like a rare, giant, fire-colored lily.

We called ourselves the usual suspects: my best friend, Ell, who I had met in a recovery meeting and who had survived their own struggles with grace and grit, and Heidi, a mom to a lovely daughter who was soon returning to our city from an inpatient treatment program in Arizona. Heidi was terrified when her daughter, an honor roll student and exceptionally talented artist, had gotten involved with hard drugs. She woke up to a phone call one night: her daughter had passed out and almost died choking on her own vomit after her second time doing heroin.

We were three people deeply connected to the mission and vision and passion of what we were doing. I could feel the words of Matthew 18:20 in my blood as we sat and strategized and built a nonprofit from the ground up with no experience whatsoever: *for where two or three gather in my name, there am I with them.* Alex's life and death also reminded me that *she* needed a home—all of the Alex's—somewhere to be safe and healthy; a safe haven to heal.

We spent countless evenings and weekends on our laptops at Panera Bread and Starbucks and a great little take-out Thai place where most people just came in to get their food and take it home. But we loved to sit there and talk and plan and scheme and listen to old brass band music.

It was an amazing journey seeing this dream come to fruition. From the building and fundraising to opening doors and then merging with another organization a couple years later—it all started with a mustard seed-sized dream. The day we opened the doors of the sky blue, three-story 1920s house for four women who needed a place to stay sober in the community, we sat in the office room where there was a poster of a mountain and a climber scaling its rocky heights that said: "Possibility." Huddled together, I asked if I could say a prayer.

I thanked God for the dream, the hard work, and the vision. I thanked God that my sober friends had not let the tiny fire in my heart burn out. I thanked God for Florence, who had helped encourage and equip me with boldness. I thanked God for the person that had connected Ell and I to Heidi. We asked God for a couple simple things:

"Lord, be in the place. Be a light for these women. Connect them and let them feel your love and peace. Heal them. And let this place feel like home for them—a safe place, a shelter in the storm."

If it was not for this dream and for this opportunity to give back, I'm not sure where I would be today. Recovery is giving back. It is stepping outside of yourself to walk alongside someone who needs you for a time to shine your light until they get theirs back. It's how little pieces of self-forgetting can step in and save us from ourselves.

At Connect House, we saw women change. We saw them find recovery and falter; find recovery and gain strength; find recovery and find themselves. But we also saw the tragic reality of addiction: the recurrence of use (one of the symptoms of the disease of addiction), broken and breaking family relationships, and even death. But through it all, we offered an open door and every time I sat outside on the front porch with one of the residents, laughing or crying, I felt Alex smile and Jesus' whisper: "Yes."

We also saw the radical power of grace and vulnerability. The way that a shift of perspective can heal old wounds.

Every Thanksgiving at Connect House we had a special dinner for the residents. We cut vegetables in the kitchen, lit candles, laughed and talked about recovery and relationships. Some of the ladies went home for the holidays, but some did not have a home or family to return to, so we wanted to make sure that there was a time and place for everyone to celebrate. We wanted the smell of turkey (or tofurky), gravy, blueberry pie and pumpkin bars to drift through the house. We wanted every woman to be unconditionally loved. Not just feel loved, but to know love.

On one of these Thanksgiving dinners, the women circled the round oak table filled with pretty bowls of steaming food, smiling. Light filtered into the northern facing window and through half-drawn, white-sheer drapes onto the mint green walls, giving life to rows of small potted plants that Madeline had painstakingly potted one-by-one. She stood, holding a dish and smiling proudly with her long braids like a crown. She smiled, little lines like badges of honor appearing around her eyes and mouth.

The residents all thought I was a bit sappy (their word) and probably a bit awkward and a bit too forthcoming with parts of my story at times, yet I could tell that most of them, over time, grew to have the same appreciation as I did for rigorous honesty and vulnerability. If I could share only one thing with them, it would be this: Don't run from your pain or hide it. Bring it out into the light. All of it. Every gritty, sleazy, shameful thing.

As a tradition, we had a gratitude circle at the start of every holiday meal and ended it with what we were grateful for at the end of every weekly check-in. The women, including myself, went around the table and shared one good thing and one not so good thing that we were grateful for. It was important to me that we encouraged the women to look at all the circumstances of their lives with thanksgiving—even the ugly parts—like I had learned through my own experience (and continue to learn on a daily basis). The circle went something like this:

"I am thankful for family and addiction."

"I am grateful for my recovery and neglect."

"This meal and abuse."

"I am grateful for meetings and homelessness."

"Sponsors and divorce."

"I am so thankful for my pet dog and for the times I was raped."

Hearing the words of each woman was so intense and gritty and real—and also so healing and affirming and life-giving. The juxtaposition of joy and sorrow all held together by the gift of gratitude that only recovery and healing—even slow, excruciating healing—can bring. By the time we were ready to eat (and by this time starving and ready to dive in to that stuffing and mashed potatoes with gravy!), there was a lightness in the room that you could almost taste. Even the walls of the room, already bright, appeared to brighten even more. The feeling tasted sweet.

Chapter 13:

BROKEN, UNBROKEN PROMISES

For a compassionate person nothing human is alien:
no joy and no sorrow, no way of living and no way of dying.
— Henri Nouwen

ecovery is defined "as a process of change through which individuals improve their health and wellness, live self-directed lives, and strive to reach their full potential," according to the Substance Abuse and Mental Health Services Administration (SAMHSA), which is a federal agency that oversees billions of dollars annually to address issues related to addiction and mental health within the US Department of Health and Human Services. Additionally, SAMHSA notes that "recovery is built on access to evidence-based clinical treatment and recovery support services." A dimension of recovery that is recognized across the addiction recovery field as integral to supporting a healthy recovery from addiction and other challenges includes home—or having a stable and safe place to live.[52]

The fact that we all need somewhere safe to live in order to thrive doesn't take a social scientist or federal agency to determine. It doesn't matter if addiction is your thing or not. Everyone needs a place where they feel safe and supported; a place to lay our heads at night in peace. For those of us with trauma histories (and remember, some studies show that this is over 80% of women with addiction issues) who are already feeling unsafe even when we have a roof over our head, a safe place to go to is critical. It can mean life or death for women leaving addiction treatment or incarceration, women seeking transformation.

In scripture, God speaks through the prophet Isaiah in Isaiah 58:6-8. He talks about the kind of fasting that God requires. It is not the limiting of food or drink (although this may have its time and place and more power to you!), but about serving others. I've learned that when I do this, when I work to "to set the oppressed free and break every yoke," something miraculous happens: my own life gets a little brighter and the darkness subsides, even if only a tiny bit at a time.

Helping others to become free from addiction can look like so many things. It can be picking up cigarette butts outside of meetings and otherwise clean-looking church yards; it can be refilling coffee pots and making sure the newcomer knows what room to go to; it can be calling someone who you know is struggling or dropping off a fresh loaf of bread just because; it can be sending birthday cards or congratulatory notes or showing up when babies are born or grandparents pass. Helping others is being there for all of the big and little moments. The celebrations and the quiet angst of life. It doesn't have to be starting a nonprofit recovery home or other recovery support service (though it surely can be!). Sharing our experience, strength, and hope is all that is required. Working to bring freedom to those who are captive to addiction or trauma or other challenges, in whatever form, is all that is needed.

When people like myself and Madeline are encouraged to put the substances down and show up in simple ways for others, something incredible happens. Not only are the people we are working with helped. It is the encourager, as Isaiah states in these passages, that is healed. If you work to alleviate the suffering of others, your healing will also quickly appear. Isaiah continues:

> *Your healing will spring up quickly; when you help heal the hurting and brokenness in others, you receive healing too. Your gloom will be like the noonday.*[53]

Memories of Madeline make me smile, though her road hasn't always been easy, even after finding recovery again. There are other women, too, women like Alex whose memory lights my soul, but also sets it on fire. I'm angry at a system that feeds pills to young people and then is astonished when these young people turn to heroin because it is cheaper and easier to find. Without some form of opiate in their system, they twist and writhe in pain, sick like someone with cancer who is undergoing radiation. It makes me angry at the perpetrators of trauma and how their actions can be the catalyst for entire lives wasted. Possibility vanished. If you have any doubts about this, just visit a detox center and take a big, deep breath in through your nose and look around. There are so many reasons to step up and show up for all people seeking recovery.

The coffee shop was dimly lit and I stared at the half-empty latte in front of me. I was very early, even for me, needing to find the perfect spot so I could feel as comfortable as I could—something that I learned over time helped quite a bit when I struggled with anxiety. When I was feeling nervous or itchy in social situations, not knowing what to expect, something as simple as choosing where I was going to sit helped. Soft classical piano played in the background, maybe Chopin. I remembered how I loved to play "Für Elise" on a keyboard when I was young. One of the only songs—besides "The Entertainer"—that I'd ever learn how to play. She walked in and instantly I knew it was her.

Florence's eyes were strong, yet soft, a deep green that you could get lost in and at the same time, see yourself. She told me about the work that she did, teaching a class on substance use disorders and about the years of experience she had working with women with substance use disorders and trauma histories—women like me.

"We don't say 'substance abuse' anymore."

Florence had a way (and still does) of teaching me something every time we met. This first meeting she taught me about some things about recovery I hadn't really given much thought to.

"Did you know that the way that we talk about addiction matters? The word *abuse* has such heavy, negative connotations. For some of us, it even triggers things. Especially for women in recovery. Or the word 'dirty.' Think about it. People talk about having 'dirty urines' when they are getting screening for probation or parole. Being clean or dirty. I hear the word 'dirty' and I think 'bad.' It's like we've almost been conditioned, by the way we talk about it, to see addiction as something it's not. A moral failing. A weakness. When it is really a medical condition like diabetes or cancer or heart disease."

I'd learn that once she got going, Florence could talk for hours about the things she cares about.

This—this is what I want to learn more about, I remember thinking to myself as she spoke and told me about her own recovery journey. Our stories were different in some ways, but in most ways the same themes—pain, isolation and fear—wove throughout. Then, surrender, redemption, and community. I drank in every word. She did most of the talking, but when I did speak, I could tell that she was really listening. *Really* listening. I could tell that she could really hear me.

I told her that I was thinking about and struggling with going back to college and working in the women's recovery home. She just nodded as I spoke about the research I'd done, learning about how there was a lack of affordable, safe housing for people leaving treatment and trying to maintain their recoveries. Especially for women. I told her how hard it was for me, impossible in fact, to stay sober when I got out of treatment the first time and had to return right back to the same environment, same friends, same home where I had gotten sick. How I felt called to be part of a solution to a problem I was just starting to see.

"Returning from treatment or incarceration is such a pivotal moment."

I nodded. "I'm not sure how this is all going to work out, but I know I'm supposed to be doing this."

Florence was one of the first women to swoop me up. She was someone who believed in me until I had the confidence and boldness to believe in myself. She was someone who really saw and understood that little girl sneaking beers from her grandfather's fridge, the teen needing somewhere to go after treatment, and the young adult trying to find her sober life and purpose.

As a thirty-year-old in recovery and only a couple years sober at the time, I also had so much of what I'll just call "feeling" bubbling up to the surface. Raw emotion. It felt like my skin dissolved, all of my organs exposed and pulsating for all the world to see. Everything was complicated and I knew I needed someone else to help me sort through it all. A Marie Kondo, of sorts, for my soul.

What I saw when I looked at my life and recovery looked like a Salvador Dalí painting: warped with dripping clocks and sad skylines. What Florence saw (and what she helped me to see) was the softness of my life: the sweet brush strokes and pastel impressions of a Monet—the beauty. For so long, I felt like I was the only one to experience trauma, addiction, grief and loss. She helped me to see the truth that I was just one of many. Not a special snowflake, but part of an avalanche of struggle. And this was a very comforting thought. If I was just one of many, this meant I was not alone.

I finally belonged.

When we met, I was also still struggling with searching for love in all the wrong places (this was a famous song for a reason) with all the wrong misters. I had left a life of alcohol and drug towards transformation with resolve and a face set like flint, but then the world came around and I faltered. My old coping mechanisms resurfaced and it was clear that I wasn't done learning. In the faith I thought I was ready for solid food, but in fact I was still drinking a juice box.

I started dating a man that brought out the worst in me, similar to the kind of man that I dated when I was using substances, someone that did not deserve me. I gave away too much of myself again because I did not yet have the boundaries or the self-worth or the practice to know that my body was a temple and I could say "no." The boundaries I did have were like that temporary orange fencing around construction sites: easily trampled.

When I was about twenty-seven, I bought myself a purity ring. It was quaint and had tiny words etched in cursive like "I am pure" and "I'm waiting on God". It is the kind of ring that fresh-faced twelve-year-olds get in Christian households for Christmas.

I had such pride in this ring and in my firm resolve to make sure that I was going to save "it" for marriage (this time). That's what good Christian girls do. And I desperately wanted to be a part of the in-crowd. You know, the cool Christian girl crowd. The one who totes her highlighted Bible to Christian book club, small group, and women's ministry events with tea and other stuff I never knew existed, like Lauren Daigle music and trendy head scarf wraps paired with dangling earrings.

Then I met Beau and everything went downhill fast. Shame came back.

He was a farm-loving, Wrangler-wearing Harley rider who loved to drink beer and smoke Marlboros (casually). Beau decided that an overnight camping trip in northern Wisconsin off the coast of Door County in the luminescent-orange of Midwestern fall was a good idea.

Of course, I agreed.

And left my purity ring at home.

His Harley swerved along the autumn-lined roads. The air smelled like apple crisp and his black leather jacket. At night, there were so many stars. It was like a summer night of fireflies in a corn field had fallen on its head. The twinkling captured me. I felt close to God—yet, at the same time, so far away. I could feel Him in the trees and in the starry night, but as Beau and I rode back to the campsite after having some beers at a restaurant on the first night of the trip—and then stopping to pick up a bottle for the fire—what I felt of God disappeared in an instant.

It would be okay if I just checked back in with Him in the morning, right?

Right?

So, there I was again, back to asking God to forgive me and not quite knowing what I was doing and not quite doing what I wanted to do—again.

In the Bible, I'd read about the Apostle Paul and his struggle, too: "I do not understand what I do. For what I want to do I do not do, but what I hate I do."[54]

Now, if you want an in-depth look at this passage from the Bible, I can't help you today, although maybe someone like Beth Moore can.

What I can tell you is that Beau was that something that I didn't want to do, but did anyways. Relapsing, or having a recurrence of use with alcohol after three years in recovery, might have had something to do with it, too. But I'm not blaming the booze. I take full responsibility for my weakness for men in Wranglers.

Either way, the little silver promise I tried to hold too tight was gone. I wrecked it. Again. My past, my brokenness, (some would say) my sin, kept coming back again and again and again, no matter how hard I tried to escape it. And the shame I felt because of it all was overwhelming. Any purpose that I felt smoldering, the notion that God had a plan for me, and that there was a place for me in the faith community, also extinguished. Again.

What was it about my past and my experience that kept me in this cycle, especially around sex and men? Why did any sense of purpose for my life always get confused with someone I was dating and trying not to sleep with?

If you are uncomfortable right now, I'm sorry.

Well, actually I'm not.

I think it's time to get uncomfortable.

Now, I'm not going to get all Francis Chan on you or encourage you to sell your house in the suburbs or go barefoot (although this is all awesome). What I am going to say is that I think it's time to start having difficult conversations.

For many of us, especially women, we feel alone and isolated in our experience of struggling with sex. Having it, not having it, or having too much. Being traumatized by it. Being swallowed up in objectification. Being confused by the sexuality portrayed in our culture. Not being able to buy shorts that don't show our booties (even at four years old). Not being able to follow a musical artist on Instagram without wondering if the pics and videos are considered porn. Lord, have mercy.

God has not called us to have comfortable conversations.

God has called us to life-change.

To shocking vulnerability.

To radical service.

Florence helped me to see that, even though I was still figuring it out, there was worth and something precious inside of me (and guess what? It had always been there). Not only could I say no, but I could scream it so loudly that the world could hear it like an emergency alert blasting on a city of cell phones. Even if I made mistakes, as long as the Earth circled back around to day, I could turn and go another way. A brighter one. And what is more, it was okay to talk about it. It was okay to get vulnerable and real. To break the cycle and get free. In fact, I needed to talk about it. I had to.

After I met Florence, it was only a short time until I finally said goodbye to this little girl inside of me and these toxic relationships for good. It's amazing what the love of another woman—a sister— can do.

One of the things that I love about recovery is that it's a *we* thing. We can do all the work, read all the books, go to all the counseling, sing all the Psalms, work with others and be of service, but it isn't until we sit across from a woman (or man) who has been there and can listen and can speak life to us that we truly hear for the first time. God was in those green eyes. And still is.

Today, Florence is one of my very best friends, my Ananias: a mother, sister, friend and mentor all wrapped in to one, depending on what the day brings. We live miles away from each other now, but each time we talk or vent or celebrate or mourn, our bond strengthens. Because of her, I am here. And I am not alone. There are hundreds and thousands and millions of Florence's that sip their coffee and talk and tell stories and share experiences, strength and hope as we dream and cry and change our lives.

Chapter 14:
ME, TOO

Where you go, I will go, and where you stay, I will stay. Your
people will be my people and your God my God.
– Ruth 1:16

Addiction recovery advocacy supports multiple pathways to finding and sustaining a life of recovery. I love this concept because there is so much in this world that is exclusive. When I hear the phrase, I picture one of my favorite wooded parks in Michigan, where there is a point in a particular trail that offers multiple ways to go next. If I go to the right, the path leads to a narrow boardwalk across a mile of marsh where herons and egrets like to walk slowly about like feathered ballerinas on tiptoe in those binding shoes. If I go left, there is another path that leads to more forest with thick brambles, where the trail ends and you're not sure if that's a deer-made path or if you should turn around. And finally, if I keep going straight ahead, the path leads to a hexagonal bench in the middle of another marsh. People have sat here for years, the weathered wood changing from tan to brown to slightly green, with etches carved like tattoos in the wood: like "J + C," I (heart shape) you, and just the name "Jonas."

While I totally support multiple pathways and am encouraged by the way most of the recovery community embraces this, I have started to feel like sometimes in our oddly singular emphasis on multiple pathways, we don't share enough about the specific pathways that have worked for us. That's partly why I'm writing this book. In particular, for me, the faith path (though winding and laden with doubt) is something that I want to see more of because that has been my experience: healing in recovery through the path of faith that is walked in community with others. That's also why I want to include scripture references and stories from the Bible in this winding narrative nonfiction account. In so many of the books known today as "Quit Lit"—this is missing. Faith is nowhere to be found, even when a relationship and encounter with God is central to someone's story. And Jesus—well, in some recovery circles just saying His name is like saying a cuss word (one of the very foul ones) or like bringing up harm reduction and needle exchanges (if you don't know what I'm talking about, look it up). Many believe you shouldn't say it, even if you want to say it. If this particular pathway hasn't been for you in the past, I hope you've made it this far in the book. It wasn't for me, either. And somedays, for different reasons, still isn't.

In this spirit of highlighting this particular pathway (that does, interestingly, include so many of the others—but this is another conversation), I'd like to share another story from scripture.

There are only two books in the Bible that are titled with a woman's name: Ruth and Esther. This does not speak to how God feels about women (there are lots of other scripture references affirming that, to Him, there is neither male nor female – that all are one in Christ[55]). But because there are only these two books, I thought it fitting to spend some time in at least one of them. The book of Ruth, in particular, illuminates concepts that are very important to take to heart for women and especially women like me who have struggled with addiction and trauma.

Ruth is a Moabite woman who will be the great grandmother of David (the dude that wrote a lot of Psalms and fought Goliath and had a scandalous affair and who God still loved deeply), and an ancestor of the one and only, Jesus. It's important to note that she is not Jewish; the Israelites actually looked down on Moab. The time period when the story of Ruth takes place was, culturally, not unlike our contemporary one, in some respects. It was during the time of judges and characterized "as a period of religious and moral degeneracy, national disunity, and frequent foreign oppression."[56] However, Ruth was also set during a time when there was peace between Israel and Moab, despite how they might have felt about one another.

I love how Ruth is from Moab. She is not one of God's chosen from Israel, yet still, like the Gentiles later on in history, God works through her to not only speak of His love and faithfulness for humanity through her simple actions, but also to provide a direct lineage to the Son of Man, Jesus himself. The story is centered on Ruth's loyalty to her mother-in-law, Naomi, who loses her husband and her sons, one of them being Ruth's deceased husband. Ruth follows Naomi into an unknown land among strangers. Why did Ruth do this? Because for her, it was the right thing to do. She wanted to be there to support her mother-in-law.

Boaz is another family member who offers help. He shares the leftovers of some of his crops to help Ruth and Naomi as they try to piece together their new life amid the grief. God provides a partner for Ruth and someone to ensure that Naomi will be provided for in her old age. Boaz stepped up to care for both women and ends up marrying Ruth. The book highlights how, even though the society was unraveling at the seams like a hundred-year-old area rug, a flame of love and loyalty and faithfulness between people and nations still flickered.

While there are many pictures of selfless love throughout this simple story, what stands out to me now is how female friendship is highlighted between the two women. Interestingly, conversation, let alone support of any kind between women, is rarely highlighted in scripture. Wendy Amsellem, a faculty at Drisha Institute for Jewish Education, also agrees. She notes that "Sarah and Rebecca never speak to another woman in Genesis. Rachel and Leah speak with one another just once. Deena, Jacob's daughter, never speaks at all. In the book of Esther, she speaks often, and with power, but never to another woman." Women in the Bible are often portrayed as disconnected from one another. Amsellem goes on to state that "against this background, the book of Ruth stands out as a celebration of female friendship."[57]

At first, Naomi is bitter (what her name actually means) and does not see why Ruth should want to follow her.[58] In fact, her other daughter-in-law, Orpah, returns home as soon as she has the opportunity. But Ruth stands in contrast as someone who will stand by her mother-in-law no matter what. Ruth boldly proclaims her loyalty:

Wherever you go, I will go; wherever you lodge, I will lodge: your people are my people; and your God is my God.[59]

It's not about what she can get from Naomi—it's about what she can give; and this is truly remarkable considering the pain and grief she experienced after losing her husband. Later in the story, she also selflessly gives Naomi the barley that Boaz gives to her. Naomi, wanting to show kindness in turn, provides Ruth with an opportunity to marry again. Eventually, Ruth even has a son. Both women care for each other in tangible ways. Love is depicted through selfless and practical action on both sides, not in empty words or promises or intentions.

One of the most interesting aspects of this story is that God is not mentioned often; the LORD is more an afterthought, or at least is at first glance. This book *shows* God—just like the actions of these women proved their love for one another. As is stated later in the New Testament in 1 John 3:18: "Dear children, let us know love with words or speech but with actions and in truth."

Despite her grief, living in extreme poverty, and not knowing what following her mother-in-law to a strange land would bring, Ruth shows (and does not tell) how she is full of faith that God has a purpose for their lives. I wonder in her prayers if she heard God's still, quiet voice whispering to her that all would be well. Or did she just need to rest on the shoulders of Naomi's faith, a faith that was more seasoned? After all that death, Ruth heard that God was providing for those living in Bethlehem and just like that, her bags were packed. Even if she did doubt or was afraid, Naomi was there to walk alongside her on the dusty road.

Much of the healing I experienced early on in my recovery was on the shoulders of other women. This story resonates with me because there have been many women who have walked alongside me and reminded me of the purpose and value of my life. It was a woman in Michigan who first told me that I actually reminded her of Ruth and who graciously took me under her wing. She let me see what a godly woman was about, brought me books like *Hinds' Feet on High Places* and recognized in me a little girl who was much afraid of life, of everything, and who needed to open her heart to a God who loved her from the beginning. I was her guest on numerous occasions for tea or coffee in fancy porcelain and for family holidays where her husband stood at the head of the table and read scripture and then prayed, always with quiet tears welling as he spoke or bowed his head. Never once did I feel judged or not good enough. The only problem with how she approached me was that sometimes I felt *too* loved, *too* understood, *too* cared for—and this was disarming in a way that I so desperately needed.

And then there was Florence, the woman in recovery who taught me that I had a voice, and I could use that voice to help other women find theirs. She, like Naomi, had the faith I needed and all I had to do was trust in her belief until mine held me up. Florence helped me to break the pattern of unhealthy relationships that triggered my past trauma, the backsliding feet-first into the icky comfortableness of a broken life that no longer suited me. Not only did she mentor me, she walked alongside me as I worked with other women, too. We worked together on an advocacy project to build up and equip the recovery community in Wisconsin. We shared so much together: laughter, tears, frustration, incredulous eye rolls and "Meg Ryan Moments" (this is an inside joke of ours). Florence has been a friend and sister and my Naomi on many occasions. Her belief in me was (and still is sometimes) greater than the confidence I've had in myself.

No one knows the author of Ruth. The need for someone to get credit for this lovely story fades into the distance of what I think God intended in its reading. It is an amazing account of loyalty, love, and friendship, of what it looks like when women truly care for each other. And I think it is also the perfect picture of recovery. In recovery, the support of women is crucial. I've been there and know how God can work through us to bring healing. For some women, it is the only way we can break free from our past trauma. The only way we can begin to believe in the persistent love of God is through the persistent love of others, whether in the downstairs church or upstairs church. I love how scripture can illuminate the recovery road. Basement grace is scandalous.

Chapter 15:

SHAKING FROM MY HEART TO MY FEET

Our greatest pain and greatest joy come in relationship with others.
– Stephen Covey

W hen I was twenty-three, my mom asked me how I could afford to book a trip out to the West Coast with a boy I was dating and I just rolled my eyes. Hadn't she ever heard of Mastercard? I had a bad habit (one of many) of spending money I didn't have. I don't recall paying attention during the consumer education class in high school (or maybe I skipped that day) when they talked about debt, and more specifically, credit card debt.

Not surprisingly I spent years—yes, years—paying off the couple thousand dollars I charged for the trip (of course that particular boy never paid me back for his share). Every month I was reminded of the bad choice—or more appropriate, the series of bad choices— that went along with that week-long (mis)adventure. Probably one of the only things I don't regret about that trip is the time I got to spend with the sea.

The ocean—or even Lake Michigan, for me—has always been a spectacular immensity. It reminds me of my smallness, and in contrast, the earth's largeness and resilience. I think about the fact that the sound, like all of humanity breathing in and out through pursed lips, continues for epochs. The waves I watched back then when my hair was black like cormorant wings and I still had a sliver of that naïveté (or better, ignorance) of youth, are still moving today. If I close my eyes, I can smell the salt clouds, hear the seals bellow on the jagged rocks in the distance, and see how the line of the horizon melts and stretches a limitless turquoise forever.

On this regrettably expensive trip, I spent a lot of time sitting on an overlook at a small motel we found while driving south down U.S. Highway 101 from Portland. I laugh now, but we had decided to just "wing it" (ah, one of the privileges of having no dependents). We landed in a big unfamiliar city, rented a car (I'm still not sure why they let you rent a car before your brain is fully developed), and just drove. As we moved along, the landscape shifted in and out of the sand-lined coast, and as we came around the next bend, the world opened up to the most expansive, beautiful scene with foggy boulders that jutted out here and there as if some Greek goddess had flung them and forgotten.

After a couple hours driving along, we passed a series of sky-blue houses dotting the ledge of one of the expansive views, and I told the boy to stop. This was it. We unloaded the few bags we brought with us and nestled in to the old motel with outdated beachy décor. The rest of the trip was taking little day trips from our new home base: riding horses on the beach at sunset, seeing other coastal cities, and hiking. No offense to the boy, but it is hard for me to think there was anyone else with me when I look back on this trip because all

I felt was a pleasant solitude with this other presence right next to me—the ocean.

The boy I was with, thankfully, liked to spend time alone, too, and met a native west-coaster at the motel and they did what boys do and probably smoked a lot of pot while I was able to take a little notebook and sit at my overlook. I still have that little book with scribbles in it, describing how I felt connected with the sea, how I could almost hear God's whisper there, how it made me feel like home—something I had been searching for a long, long time.

Looking out over the waves also had a tendency to make me remember things that I'd rather forget. As if the movement of the water carries me back. Things I've done, and things that have happened to me. This trip was no different. As I sat on my little grassy spot with my little notebook in the dewy mist of the early morning or right as the sun was falling into the lavender water at dusk, I wrote about some of the things I had come through and how I ended up sitting where I was at that particular moment in time. I hadn't yet been moved by my experiences at church or in a recovery community; I hadn't yet learned the skills—like deep breathing, prayer, walking, writing, hanging with my puppy and talking to my lady friends—that would later become so very important to helping me cope with my trauma responses. But I sensed there was something powerful happening in those moments when a pen was in my hand, dancing across the tear-streaked page.

When I think of the word resilience, I think about the sea or lakes and how the waters move, no matter what: in and out, back and forth, carrying its heaviness into the shoreline and then back out to the horizon again. There is this calm, even when the winds gust and the waves crash, like God is breathing two simple words through this part of creation: keep going.

No matter what, keep going.

The day I wrote the last check (back when we wrote things called checks) to pay off the trip, I let out a big ocean-style exhale. I had stuck with it and finally my debt had been paid.

In the book of James in the Bible, James talks about how we can "consider it pure joy" when we face trials because this is how perseverance is grown.[60] Like one of Madeline's little seedlings in the window, it is tenderly cared for and watered by trial. The ability to endure, to be resilient, to keep going—these skills are forged in the tough times in life. Like the waves, we can keep moving no matter what. And then, if we persevere, the joy we feel on the other side; our bright stories of resilience.

Damascus Road Church (great name) sends buses out in the morning to pick people up from nearby inpatient addiction treatment centers. The service was held in a sanctuary that used to be a car show-room. The white floors glistened and a wall of windows was covered by hand-sewn black drapes that kept the glare out. If you haven't been to church in a while, I don't want to freak you out, but Christians in most nations today do church pretty much anywhere. Gymnasiums, around flag poles, vacant bars, basements, bomb shelters.

I went to several women's ministry events there, one being a candlelit tea with disgustingly feminine décor. Round tables with floral and gold accents or accessories and doodads and other sparkly things. We sang and shared in our small, floral circles, answering icebreaker questions that were printed on small note cards in colors that matched the tablecloths. The conversation was pleasant enough, but no one was getting too deep with each other yet. Unlike the grit of a recovery meeting, church was too quiet, too sterile. Like hanging out with a bunch of people who are afraid to dance.

Until all of a sudden, a woman in the congregation jogged to the front of the room wearing an over-sized white sweatsuit. It took me a minute to realize what was written on the material with large black and red letters as she approached center stage. As she got closer, it came into focus. The words formed into every combination of every horrible thing I had ever been called or thought about myself:

worthless,

abused,

broken,

dirty,

shameful,

slut,

liar,

fraud,

not good enough,

never good enough,

fat,

ugly,

horrible,

whore...

This woman went on to share her testimony about being sexually abused as a child by a family member. It went on for years. As she spoke, I felt myself melting into my chair, biting the inside of my mouth (something I had learned subconsciously to do as a way to not disassociate and have flashbacks of my own). People talking about trauma can be very traumatizing for those who have experienced it. You may understand what I mean.

Deep breath.

She talked about what she experienced and also what she learned from her sufferings.

"I felt so dirty and shameful for years. Like I had this giant secret that was so bad it made me a bad person. And what is worse, I felt like I couldn't tell anyone because it was my fault."

Deep breath.

"But somehow, I learned that God was present and I was still loved. Even if I did not understand why this happened. It didn't have to make sense. God still loved and cared for me. Miraculously. Beautifully. To Jesus, I have always been a queen."

She jogged back to her seat with a smile. Some of us looked at her with compassion or pity and some of us looked towards the ground. There were many hands reaching in purses for Kleenex or passing it around. Women are generous with their tissues. Then, standing by her chair, she pulled off the clothes covered in all of those words of shame and filth and underneath was a pretty purple blouse and blue jeans. I looked towards her again. She smiled at me as our eyes touched. Then the leader stood up and asked us to get the cards that were tucked into the pocket of our folders.

"If you feel comfortable and are able, I invite you to stand. Take your card and let's say this together. Where there is a blank spot in the beginning, say your name."

The room was quiet a moment and I looked down at the card in my hands. Then the chorus began:

I am _ (your name).

I am a party waiting to happen, 1 Peter 1:8. Angels rejoice over me, demons flee from me, James 4:7, and God himself dances over me with singing, Zephaniah 3:17. I am: the bearer of good news, Isaiah 52:7, a minister of reconciliation, 2 Corinthians 5:18, the carrier of the King of Glory, Colossians 1:27. I am the righteousness of Christ, 2 Corinthians 5:21, and the a temple of the Holy Spirit, 1 Corinthians 6:19. I have an unction from the Holy One and know all things, 1 John 2:20. I have the mind of Christ, 1 Corinthians 2:16, I am anointed by God, 1 John 2:27, and I was created by Him for good works, Ephesians 2:10! I have favor with God, favor with man, and a good understanding, Luke 2:52. I am chosen by God, John 15:16, Ephesians 1:4, I have been sanctified, 1 Corinthians 6:11, and made truly Holy. As Jesus is, so am I in this world, 1 John 4:17! I am always on God's mind, He thinks about me constantly, Psalm 139:17-18. Even before the creation of the world, I was planned, Ephesians 1:4. I am a child of the King, adopted into his family, Ephesians 1:5, an heir in Christ, Romans 8:17, accepted in the Beloved, Ephesians 1:6. I am blessed with every spiritual blessing in heavenly places, Ephesians 1:3. I lack no good thing, Psalm 34:10. I have an abundance for every good work, 2 Corinthians 9:8. I was predestined by God for success, Romans 8:28-30. I am placed and seated with Him, a king and priest, part of a chosen generation, a peculiar people, 1 Peter 2:9. I am blessed coming in and going out, Deuteronomy 28:6.My family is blessed, Deuteronomy 28:4, and everything I touch prospers, Deuteronomy 28:8. I am the head and not the tail, above the circumstances and not beneath them, Deuteronomy 28:13. No weapon formed against me can prosper, Isaiah 54:17, no plague can come near my dwelling—my house or my body, Psalm 91:10! And nothing can separate me from the love of God—not angels or demons, not principalities or powers, nothing in this world or out of it, Romans 8:38-39! I am equipped with the full armor of God, Ephesians 6:13, packed full of the Holy Spirit, with more than enough power inside of me to raise the dead, Romans 8:11, heal the sick and cast out devils, Matthew 10:1.

My faith can move mountains, Mark 11:23, my words contain life and death, Proverbs 18:21, my life was bought at a price— Jesus covered it, 1 Corinthians 6:20. My days are appointed, Psalm 139:16, my life is protected, Mark 16:18, angels encamp around me, Psalm 34:7, and the blessings of God encircle me, Psalm 103:4.Go before me and overtake me, Deuteronomy 28:2. The creator of the universe, Dad, loves me with an everlasting love, Jeremiah 31:3. He is with me always, Hebrews 13: 5, He thinks about me constantly, Psalm 139:17. He knows everything about me, even the numbers of hairs on my head, Matthew 10:30. His love for me is inescapable, insurmountable and irrefutable. I am all around awesome, just ask my Dad![61]

When we finished, there were shouts and claps and hips swaying and hands raised. There was sobbing. Mine. I was crying uncontrollably and shaking from my heart to my feet. Women gathered around me and put their gentle hands on my back and shoulders and started to pray. I heard things whispered like "Praise, Jesus" and "Amen" and "Give her strength" and "Show her your love for her."

Brennan Manning in the *Wisdom of Tenderness* writes:

Whether your childhood was idyllic or abusive, the challenge stands: Do you accept yourself as one utterly loved by God? The human love experienced in a happy home, though rich and rewarding, isn't even remotely comparable to divine love, and the absolute deprivation of human affection isn't an insuperable impediment to "being seized by the power of a great affection." Both those who have been loved well and those who have known nothing but contempt in the home need stubborn grace to make the leap of faith into the arms of love.[62]

Our chorus of women proclaimed together the truth of who we were—who we are in Christ. I got vulnerable in that room of church ladies. Even if they hadn't experienced a measure of the same suffering I did, perhaps they could relate to the feeling that this suffering brought. Even if they hadn't experienced sexual violence, they could relate to the lies: "I'm got good enough, I'm broken, I'm bad or somehow beyond repair. I'm too much for God." Just like I needed these women to show me the truth of how valued and loved I really was by God, they needed me just the same.

On my own dusty road to Damascus, I've learned that my Naomi's and my Ruth's, some I've met and some I've yet to meet, are ready to dance and sing and cry and hold me up when I can't stand and sit me down when I need to be still. In recovery—in the basement and upstairs in the pews—they've shown up in their imperfect and quietly powerful ways and provided the magic ingredient of resilience: connection.

Chapter 16:
GRASS-STAINED JESUS GROUPIES

God sets the lonely in families,
he leads out the prisoners with singing...
– Psalms 68:6

On New Year's Eve of 2012, I celebrated almost one year sober and thirteen years since my near fatal overdose at the supple age of seventeen. As anyone in recovery knows, we celebrate our birthdays or the day that we started on the recovery path. Most people have a series of birthdays just as often, especially early on—there can be any number of recurrences of use that begins the clock of rebirth again. For better or worse, it is one of our customs and I go along with it because I know how encouraging it was for me to see the women with five, ten, fifteen, twenty, thirty, even forty years in recovery get their shiny coins or give their humble speeches about how they could not have done it except for the support of other women and God. That and I love a nice slice of chocolate cake and lots of these celebrations have toxic amounts of sweets—just my kind of party.

Connections Counseling, where I had met Alex, was hosting a lavish New Year's dance and I was terrified. I never felt comfortable dancing, never in my life, not drunk or even on the drugs that were supposed to make you feel like a dancing queen. Once I even went to a Limp Bizkit concert (insert: eye roll—yours and mine) on ecstasy and didn't stand up once, except to find some water. I was terrified to go to this sober event and so I did what any respectable and newly sober woman did—I tried to dig up the most "going clubbing" outfit I could find in my closet: a black sequin tank top I'd never worn but bought on a whim with a tight gray skirt. I worked zero-dollar clothing budget magic and added a belt, tights and red lipstick and looked in the mirror and thought I looked pretty decent for someone who was sober.

I arrived by myself and scanned the room for the people I knew from group: Tanya, Emily, Ell, Rachel, Suzanne, Allen. There were tables of food and cookies someone's mom dropped off and twenty bottles of sparkling grape juice. *Thank God there is a smoking section*, I thought, terribly nervous to be doing anything, let alone this mocktail event. It was horrible—until some of us gravitated towards each other in our shared awkwardness.

We started dancing.

One of the group members from Connections was a DJ who donated his time, brought all of his equipment, including flashing rainbow lights. It felt like a real live dance floor. He was a dapper fellow, like Don Draper from *Mad Men*, only not a jerk. He played music that I know was cool at the time, but I was not quite cool enough, so I had never heard it. The party was amazing and once I shed my skin of over-the-top self-consciousness and ate some of the fresh mom-baked cookies, the beats made me move like I was born that way (even though I wasn't).

I'm not sure why I thought back then that because it was a sober party, it would include counterfeit items and décor, a strobe light that only looked like a strobe light, for instance. How did sober people party or have fun anyways?

At certain points (an introvert in recovery as well), I pulled people by the hand, encouraging them to join the circle as we shook our heads and hair back and forth, swayed, did the Irish Jig, the lawn mower, the Floss (I think this is what it's called)—whatever felt right. The lights flashed. My fear dissolved with every beat. It was the most fun I ever had. Seriously. I was twenty-nine years old and for the first time in my life, having good old-fashioned fun. No alcohol needed. No drugs. No men I didn't really like. Shy, reserved, introverted, book-nerd, scared me dissolved a bit like Pop Rocks in your mouth. Pop: smiles; Crackle: laughter; Fizz: join me, won't you? And slowly others lost their inhibitions, too. And not in the false way that alcohol or other drugs help you to "relax"—this was the real deal. Soon all of us were moving and smiling and forgetting ourselves. It was beautiful.

This was around the same time that I started dreaming about Connect House, around the same time that I lost Alex and around the same time I met Florence. While I was thinking about how I could start giving back and sharing my recovery, feeling this spark ignite inside of me, I was also learning how to be in community with other people and be a friend to myself. A lesson God knew I needed.

I headed out to an outdoor patio where groups were again congregating and talking in smaller groups (just a side note: if you want to provide any type of addiction recovery support, make sure to have a smoking section). The air was cold but almost no one had their coats on. Dancing made our necks sticky with sweat and it felt good to step out into the almost-January air. The sky was black with pinholes of light. I breathed in and then exhaled slowly, and as I looked around, I felt a new sense of calm. Usually being in crowds, especially when men were around, made me nervous. Sometimes I had flashbacks from that night at the bar and my hands would sweat and I would feel the weight of that door being pushed into me, how it felt to realize there was nothing I could do—I was powerless.

I was still powerless—powerless over my addictions, much of my past, and my life, unmanageable as it had become—but around this powerlessness something new was being formed. A community of brokenness somehow, mysteriously, incredibly, added strength. Now, I could be with other people—even strangers—and not feel scared. I could hear music in a dark room and not see those terrible pictures in my mind anymore. I could feel tiny snowflakes hit my face and not think about him. God was doing a new thing. Again. I was in a new place now and being led in a new way.

I started to wonder if maybe God was in the business of new.

There is an interesting Ted Talk that discusses how the opposite of addiction is connection called *Everything You Think You Know About Addiction is Wrong.*[63] The basic premise of the talk is centered on an experiment with rats (choosing to be in cages with other rats instead of drinking heroin water out of a baby bottle) that shows how humans (because we are actually very similar to rats, researchers assert) need connection and will actually thrive with interaction, even with the temptation of substances like heroin.[64] British journalist Johann Hari talks about why 12 step programs and other treatment and recovery programs work. They work because they help to alleviate the isolation and loneliness that are inherent in addiction issues.

While this talk created quite the stir in the recovery world (they could have just *asked us*, instead of messing with a bunch of rats), there is truth to highlight. From my own experience, I learned this to be true: in fellowship with each other, there is life. When we open ourselves to the power of community, we open ourselves up to receive a gift. When we tell each other our deep and murky secrets, when we let others into our dark muddy pools of ick, something miraculous happens: we slowly open a door to healing. And if we don't—well, if we don't, we can stay stuck. Or worse.

Laura McKowen in *We are the Luckiest*, a memoir about her own struggle with alcoholism, says:

One stranger who understands your experience exactly will do for you what hundreds of close friends and family who don't understand cannot. It is the necessary palliative for the pain of stretching into change. It is the cool glass of water in hell.[65]

The strength and beauty and "cool glasses of water" that fellowship brings, for me, has been one of the most incredible gifts of recovery.

There is a painting called *The Return of the Prodigal Son* by the famous Baroque artist, Rembrandt. One scholar noted how the painting captured a monumental glimpse into the famous parable of the Lost Son in scripture.[66] It is a moving, tender portrait that I only learned about when researching books by Henri Nouwen, a Dutch priest whose conversion experience later in life led him to a drastic and inspiring climb down the ladder to care for people with disabilities.

Nouwen was so moved by the painting that, for several weeks, he spent hours every day contemplating the painting, which was housed in the State Hermitage Museum in St. Petersburg. Each of the men in the painting had a role: the father receiving the son who had gone off to drink and drug and sleep his way through his inheritance and the son who had stayed home "being good" and never leaving his father's side. After much time thinking about these roles Nouwen wrote:

> Rembrandt is as much the elder son of the parable as he is the younger. When, during the last years of his life, he painted both sons in *Return of the Prodigal Son*, he had lived a life in which neither the lostness of the younger son nor the lostness of the elder son was alien to him. Both needed healing and forgiveness. Both needed to come home. Both needed the embrace of a forgiving father. But from the story itself, as well as from Rembrandt's painting, it is clear that the hardest conversion to go through is the conversion of the one who stayed home.[67]

Towards the end of the book, Nouwen includes his reflections on the painting, and he talks about the invitation to joy that God asks us to receive. He notes: "Celebration belongs to God's Kingdom. God not only offers forgiveness, reconciliation, and healing, but wants to lift up these gifts as a source of joy for all who witness them."

Recovery is all about rejoicing. I learned this the first time I danced. Sober, that is. We may be the prodigals of the family, but in the end, everyone is called to conversion—a joyful heart change.

Chapter 17:

SHOW ME BRITTLE

When the jars of clay remember they are jars of clay, the treasure within gets all the glory, which seems somehow more fitting.
– Jen Hatmaker

I missed working with women after Connect House merged with a larger nonprofit. The realities of running a recovery home and the budget that goes along with it (without anything but private donations), led me to make that tough but smart choice. Although I missed the work, especially the women, I knew that God would open another door or even an egress window, if He had to, when it was time. And sure enough, it wasn't long until I had the opportunity to work for another recovery home. I was able to get a little bit of a part-time income on top of my full-time job (supporting yourself in the city as a single is almost impossible), and try to be part of something beautiful again.

This new recovery home had oak branches that loomed above it with shiny leaves that glistened in the sunlight like flecks of gold.

Within walking distance was a little mom and pop café that made the best banana bread and lattes in the winter or tart citrus-strawberry smoothies in the summer. There was also an old church that opened its doors every Monday night for a women's meeting where children were allowed. The owner of the recovery home was a kind older woman who had experienced pain of her own, and it showed in her beseeching eyes. She called all of us "girls," but no one bothered to tell her that this was a tad offensive these days.

Karissa and I drove around and smoked cigarettes. I loved going places like the pharmacy or Walmart or to a park that had a path winding along the river bank. We walked down the dusty gravel path, and on lucky days would spot one of the many eagles that soared in giant circles in the clouds with broad black wings and heads a speck of white from so far away. Driving is so disarming: you don't have to make eye contact; you can be silent. There is so much sky and movement and music between you. Car conversations with Karissa were the best and I listened quietly or talked about how tough my day was. I was real with these women. I learned this very early on in my recovery: being real is the only way to truly form a connection with another human being. Having it all together never works – and is rarely, if ever, true.

Karissa talked about her children and her mother; about how she felt so close to her brother because they had been together through everything: struggling to care for their mom every day when she got home from work and passed out with a cigarette on a borrowed couch that smelled like body odor and side-of-the-road; about her ex and how they started using heroin together; how he started beating her and how tough it was to stop using heroin and how she would rather die than leave him. How her dad died of a drug overdose. How she had to make the impossible decision to give her kids away because she knew that she wasn't well enough to take care of them—not yet.

Whenever she told me these hard-to-hear stories, I couldn't help but picture her in another life. She had long brown hair and rosy cheeks and looked like someone who should be fighting to make the cheer squad or someone who your parents hired to babysit you when you were ten years old or the clerk at the checkout counter who smiles as she hands you change or the bride walking down the aisle to her teary-eyed partner or the student studying for the MCAT or the mother driving around the silver minivan wearing yoga pants and an oversized t-shirt with milk stains.

Karissa.

So much possibility and potential.

The call came on Christmas Eve while I was visiting my then boy-friend's (soon-to-be husband's) family in Pennsylvania. My job with the recovery home meant that I was always on call day or night; if my cell phone rang, I had to answer it. I had to be ready to drop every-thing and not only answer the phone, but be there. Listen. But that night I was states away.

Karissa was in jail.

"Ok, walk me through this," I asked the other staff. "What happened?"

There was a relapse or recurrence of use. They found pills and powder and alcohol. She was overwhelmed. It had all been too much. The new job, the temptations. The men—or better, boys— were dis-tracting her and tempting her to go back. Reminding her of things that had happened. Triggering her. It was so hard to work through the trauma, to be present.

I get it.

I wanted to be there so badly, but I couldn't. I felt oceans away from her small jail cell.

We supported each other, the staff and other residents. And after countless phone calls and texts and waiting, after spending Christmas in Pennsylvania thinking about how Karissa was spending hers alone surrounded by steel bars and clanking keys and trays of stale bread and sadness, I was finally home and able to go and visit her. One of the other staff members and I drove up to the jail and checked in.

County jails in small towns are strange places. The waiting room feels sterile and smells like the principal's office. There is a white-gray speckled floor caked in the kind of dirt that you can't see unless you have to scrub the floor. There are hard, pleather covered chairs. There are flags and portraits of important people. There are clocks and alarms and signs that tell you the visiting hours, where to line up, and to have your ID ready.

When it was time, I walked into the closet-like space and picked up the receiver. She sat down across from us and cried. Her shoulders were slumped and she looked tired. The way she had started to look in recovery—walking more confidently, smiling eyes and hopeful—all of this had vanished. She was drowning in shame again.

"Karissa," I said softly and looked at her with a gentle, barely-there smile. "We love you."

She looked me in the eyes and started bawling. This wasn't the greeting she had expected.

I was quiet and nodded as she cried and apologized. I wanted so desperately to reach into the plexiglass wall and hold on to her and not let go. I wanted to let her rest her head on my shoulder and tell me all of it: her fears, her insecurities, her hopes, her dreams. I wanted to wipe away all of the pain and make it as though it never happened. I wanted to give her the grace that I had received.

All of a sudden, a red light flashed—that was the minute warning.

"We need more time," I said, but knew there was no changing it.

I reaffirmed our love for her and she shook her head and kept repeating that she was sorry. She didn't mean to. She never meant to use again. It wasn't what she wanted. I told her this can be part of the process. It wasn't over; she didn't have to start over. She could pick up right where she left off with recovery. We were all there for her.

Several months later, I went for a morning jog in the park by my house. I was preparing for a big recovery event, the recovery month rally that me and Florence and some friends had been planning and now it was the eve of the big day. I'd found that when I was feeling tense or anxious, exercise worked great to relieve some stress—way better than drugs or alcohol ever had. The air was warm for September and I noticed how the birds were still chirping like it was spring time and the light was bright. All of a sudden, I stopped. I thought I felt someone right behind me and turned but no one was there.

It was the morning she died. I'd learned later that as I was running, she was being taken off life support in the ICU. They had kept her alive long enough to be able to donate some of her organs.

When she left jail, she was not allowed to come back to the recovery home, although she desperately wanted to. It was a choice given to the other women in the home; other women who were early in recovery and felt unsafe and needed to have boundaries and needed to know there were consequences if you used. The vote was "no." She could not return. My vote had been "yes." YES.

Please.

Please let her in and don't shut her out. She needs us now more than ever! She needs a place. She needs safety. She needs a second and third and fourth and new chance every day, every second, if that's what will keep her well.

It was entirely the wrong call. I did not fight for Karissa to be able to stay. I stepped aside as the decision was made, even though I disagreed because this was their home and at the time it was the policy. The residents decided together. Now, I can't say Karissa would not have died if she came back to the recovery home. Maybe one of the other residents would have. There is no way to tell and that is not how it happened. What I can say is that she needed the opportunity. This, after all, is why recovery homes are so important: we need an unconditional safe place where there is always an open door. And always a *yes, please come home.*

When I learned of her death, I was at a fancy meeting for my day job as a recovery advocate, where politicians and other fancy people who wore ties and skirt suits and were always looking down at their cell phones were talking about the opioid crisis. I sat in the back, feeling out of place like I usually did at those meetings but wanting to be there to bring a voice of someone in recovery to the table. Despite my discomfort, there was still so much grace given by many of those fancy people. Almost everyone in the room was wholly committed to making the world where they had influence a little better for people struggling with addiction. They were using their privilege in a positive way. It was incredible to learn over time, too, that it didn't matter how fancy or what title or what income any of these people had—many of them were personally touched by addiction: their sons and daughters, mothers and fathers, neighbors, themselves.

My phone rang and I instinctively knew I had to step out and answer.

"Did you hear the news?"

I was in shock and stumbled around trying to find someone who knew her, someone to tell. I ran into two of the women who knew about the recovery home and they had already heard. ICU. Organ donation. The results of the opioid crisis reaching our phones and lives directly and stabbing our hearts over and over again. Somehow, I left the building after the meeting was over, weaving in and out of the suits and clicking heels, not wanting to make eye contact with anyone who didn't know her. All I longed for was a connection with her again.

Karissa.

I started driving home, swerving on the backroads. I had to pull over as the cries came in dry heaves, poisoned by the pain, trying to vomit all of the sadness out. I called my friend Jessica—something I had learned to do in recovery and accepted doing when I was struggling. I needed support. Right now.

"We didn't let her back in. We could have—she should still be alive...," my words broke into pieces.

One of the reasons I called Jessica is because she had been there. She is a family member of someone affected by addiction. She knew the pain of the back and forth—the sickness and healing and sickness again—the turmoil and feelings of being responsible. She knew the need to let go—the confusion of it all.

Jessica asserted there was nothing I could do. We did the right thing at the time and this was the result of her actions. She helped me to recognize that I wasn't responsible for the situation

"It's a lot easier sometimes to blame ourselves than try to sit back and figure out why God would allow such a thing when we can never figure it out. We are human. God is in control."

They've been with me when I've taken calls late at night or early in the morning from people needing treatment or parents desperate to know if there should be "tough love" and consequences or another shot at living at home. They've been with me when my church asks about starting a recovery ministry or when I venture out to try something new for my own recovery. They whisper softly. The spirits of those who leave too soon, like Alex and Karissa, maybe they work with God to guide us in opening our eyes to what is truly beautiful in the world. Maybe they help to teach us how to show others this beauty.

Maybe people like Tanya and Florence, too, who make it out alive to do hard and amazing things, are reflections of God that inspire those of us in recovery (and those who are not) to live in a new way. Even in death, God keeps showing up again and again. Fyodor Dostoevsky, a Russian novelist, said that "the world will be saved by beauty." Meeting women in recovery—those who live through it and those who pass on—has transformed and softened my heart. Made it beautiful. All of these women also remind me how persistent this beauty is if I keep my eyes open to it.

Women in recovery also show me brittle.

The Apostle Paul says:

> *But we have this treasure in jars of clay to show that this all-surpassing power is from God and not from us. We are hard pressed on every side, but not crushed; perplexed, but not in despair; persecuted, but not abandoned; struck down, but not destroyed (2 Corinthians 4:7-9).*

Now, you have to understand who the Corinthians were and what kind of society they lived in to really be able to let this verse sink in. And not only that, but you need to understand the types of hardships that Paul had endured up until this point that he alludes to in these verses. Paul loved the Corinthians dearly, but they were a rebellious lot who enjoyed lots of Bridgerton-style sex (of the pre-marital variety) and food and slander. You name the sin, they loved it. Their churches were unruly and confused and they were having a tough time letting the truth of grace soften their hardened hearts. They were also divided, and as scripture states and Paul knew well, *a house divided against itself cannot stand.*[68] Paul loved them dearly and wanted to make sure their faith could not only survive but thrive. After offering suggestions and warnings in 1 Corinthians, Paul wanted to follow up, as was his style. Classic Paul.

As a reformed Corinthian myself, I understand how challenging this is, especially when living in a society that offers temptations at every turn and sin sometimes looks so darn fun or tasty or handsome or all of these combined. Throw a history of trauma in there with boundary issues and self-loathing and pride, and the waters get even muddier. But Paul had received good news from Titus – Hallelujah! – the Corinthians were learning and loving like he had taught, how Jesus had taught him. He had a lot to celebrate with them, but also as was Paul's style, he had much to continue to warn them about. He did not want them to become weary of doing good. He also wanted them to remain unified.

There were also believers who were questioning his legitimacy and his apostleship, so near the end of 56 AD, Paul sat down, possibly in Philippi (I like to imagine with freshly soaked feet, a clean tunic, and man-bun) and penned the remaining one of two letters to the Corinthians,[69] along with that verse.

Jars of clay were made of the earth, very breakable and basically worthless. They held water or were used for lamps and other everyday things. There is also more recent commentary that suggests these small jars were used to hold coins. Archeologists have found the remnants of clay jars with coins in Israel and Turkey; and interestingly, the word that Jesus uses to describe *treasure* in Greek is the same in these verses and in another parable in Matthew 13:44, where he talks about a man who found a collection of coins and sold everything to buy a field that contained it.[70] Whatever interpretation of "jars of clay" rings true for you, one thing is certain: what was inside the clay jar was much more valuable than the jar itself.

But we have this treasure in jars of clay to show that this all-surpassing power is from God and not from us.

"All-surpassing" is a powerful word. I can't recall anything, ever, that has been described as "all-surpassing" besides God's power. And maybe Amazon Prime. Paul loved to use the word "surpassing." You can find it in several of his letters, including the ones for the Corinthians, Philippians, and Ephesians. A psalmist and the author of Ecclesiastes loved it, too. Googling the word, I see this:

incomparable, outstanding, excelling, extraordinary, greatly exceeding others to a high degree.

Paul says that God's power is *all* of this; or, in other words, there is nothing above the power of God. The apostle wanted to make sure that his audience knew where his power came from. He was the clay jar: fragile, prone to break, utterly worthless on its own. What was amazing wasn't this little dingy thing that you wouldn't even want on your end table; what was amazing was that with the unmatchable and amazing power of God, Paul could rise above and survive a lifetime of trials and tribulations. And so can we. We are hard pressed, perplexed, persecuted and struck down; but not crushed, in despair, abandoned or destroyed.

Part 3:
BEAUTY UPSTAIRS

Chapter 18:
GET REAL (FOR REAL)

No amount of spiritual makeup can render us
more presentable to God.
– Brennan Manning

Recently I posed a question to my friends on social media, mainly women and men who are in or seeking addiction and mental health recovery. I asked:

"What is the first thing that comes to mind when you hear the word 'Christian?'"

Here is a summary of the most popular responses I got:

"Skeptical."

"Trauma."

"Hypocrite."

"Judgmental."

"Exclusion."

"Intolerant."

Of course, there were some sunny exceptions like "love" and "Jesus" and "messenger;" and even some funny answers like "Bale" (as in Christian Bale as Batman). But the prevailing tone was negative. In the words of physician Paul Tournier in *Guilt & Grace*, "...religion— mine as well as that of all believers—can crush instead of liberate." For many of my followers on social media, the idea of Christianity crushes. We have the reputation of displaying all of the most revile of characteristics, being all of these things (judgmental, hypocritical, fake) and worse.

The church is the place where these broken (I'd argue, human) folks are housed. Now, I'd like to clarify here that my intention in writing this book is not to criticize the church, but to illuminate something for it, for all of us. Shine a little light on what goes on in the basement and show what happens in the recovery world where I and so many others have felt moved by a heavenly jolt and embraced by grace. I am well aware of the plank in my eye, compared to your splinter. In fact, you've had a nice picture of my plank in the words I've shared.

The downstairs church? The radicals and misfits and ragamuffins and liars and cheaters and dealers and gluttons and tax collectors and prostitutes and women in recovery—I hate to break it to you all, but we look more like the folks Jesus came to serve and save in the first place. The ones who turned away from honesty (with themselves and others), refused to extend grace, passed by on the other side of the street so as to avoid the costly, vulnerable, holy act of compassion— these folks he condemned. Repeatedly.

Philip Yancey writes that "In his life Jesus proved that no one need fall below the reach of God's grace."[71] This is spectacular news that is good and hopeful and redeeming. No one is beyond saving. Yet how does this good news change us? How can these words move from just words into a new way of being? How can we bring the grace that we learn and receive from the downstairs church into the pews upstairs?

And—importantly—how can the upstairs church truly, really, reflect back the love of God that they have also so graciously received as a gift and treasure, too?

Lori walked into the room wearing a green business suit, legs up to her neck, thick brown hair and a face that says two things: I've been there and I'm worth it.

I knew at once that she had what I wanted.

After talking to my friends and gaining a little courage, I approached her after a meeting. When I asked if she'd like to talk, the first thing she said was "Let's pray about it."

Then Lori showed up.

It wasn't long before Lori's number in my cell phone was on the most-called (or texted) list. When I needed guidance working through a situation, I reached out. When my mind swirled like a gulf stream with obsessive or destructive thinking, I asked for help. During the most monumental joys in my recovery: getting married and then getting pregnant (with twins!), she glided alongside me, an elegant swan, while I floundered—but just a little bit less—because she was there. Gracefully, she shared her experience, strength, and hope.

At a certain point in our mentor-type relationship, she encouraged me to write a care-of-God list. This took some explaining. I understood what care was, certainly. And at the time I wanted to think I understood God just a little bit, but what did it mean to put it all together? Step 3 of Alcoholics Anonymous states that we "Made a decision to turn our will and our lives over to the *care of God* as we understood him."

She explained to me what her own mentor had encouraged her to do many years ago:

"Sit down and find a quiet place. Then think back. Write a list all of the times in your life that God showed up. All the times that the care of God was—is—evident."

My first thought: "This is going to be a long list."

I followed her direction and snuggled in to my favorite sunny spot in my favorite quiet room at just the right hour of the day. The hour when the light through the trees hits just so. Even if it isn't, the room feels warmer because of the brightness. Words cartwheeled onto the page. Images like the pages of a photograph album flipping through so many of the events of my life: my parent's divorce, my grandfather's death, sexual assault and addiction. My footprints-in-the-sand moments when I was about to slip and fall and needed carrying. When I was carried.

And the joyful moments, too: graduating college, falling in love, being of service. Trees of life that grow and flourish.

I read this list aloud—and more—to my mentor and she nodded silently and smiled.

She has a list, too.

As she listened, I was taken by the simple power of connection in being present with another human being and *really* being listened to. Lisa wasn't trying to evangelize or save my soul. She had no ulterior motive of helping me to see my arrogance or pride or slippery, sin-soaked self. Stephen Covey notes that "most people do not listen with the intent to understand; they listen with the intent to reply." Lisa, in her stillness, opened up a place of safety for me. She wasn't focused on how she was going to respond; in fact, she barely did with words. Her eyes did all the talking necessary.[72]

I'd like to blame my poor memory on "mom brain" or "Covid fog" or even smoking a little too much pot during my teens and early twenties. The truth is (while all of these things might be true) the answer is simple: I'm human. Just like the Israelites back in the day, I don't always remember my list or the countless ways that God shows up. The Israelites were a stubborn people, as related in the Old Testament. They had been helped by God again and again, spared despite their overt rebellion, yet time and time again they wandered.[73]

Time and time again. Even when I don't deserve it, and often *especially* when I don't deserve it, God swoops down with his infinite mercy and forgiving grace. In Lisa's response, I heard with my heart the words of the joyful singer: "Come and hear, all you who fear God; let me tell you what he has done for me."[74] Since that time, I've also wondered what could happen if we all took a minute to pause and reflect on the care of God in our lives. And did this regularly. In the basement recovery rooms, in the pews upstairs, in the living room, in the stadium, in the bar that turns into a hip, millennial church on Sundays. Would this change the way that we cared for others, too?

Chapter 19:
SHINE A LIGHT

If suffering alone taught, all the world would be
wise, since everyone suffers. To suffering must be
added mourning, understanding, patience, love,
openness, and the willingness to remain vulnerable."
– Anne Morrow Lindbergh

On Instagram, I recently saw a post by author and teacher Jennie Allen from the *Passion 2022* conference. Now, I have never been to such a conference, but have to admit that it was freakish, to me, how many college-aged folks gather together in a football stadium to talk about God and learn more about Jesus. Something like 60,000 of them. This was startling, but what was perhaps more startling was what I saw next.

It was a picture of the smallish-blonde woman named Jennie standing in her intentionally casual blazer and fun kicks near crates labeled "weight" and "sin." She carried two of the crates as she spoke:

"What the enemy does is build a wall of shame and what you do is hide behind it. We do little dances in front of this, but our souls, our secrets, ourselves are actually tucked behind a wall because dare we tell anyone about the..."

And then she led the students to confess. Out loud.

That's right, confess. Get it all out there. The dirty, semen-stained truth. The weight: what cannot be controlled. The sin: what can. The secrets from childhood. The lies. The conceit and pride.

When I swiped right on her post, there were pictures of students bending, arm-in-arm, in small circles. Dreadlocks, hoodies, so many perfectly manicured eyebrows, 1990s fashion (oh my), and all the other outward signs of the younger generation. But inwardly? In my mind, I imagined the shaking, the fear, then the sweet release that only honesty—radical honesty—can bring. Shining light coming out of the dark. Just like I've witnessed in addiction recovery spaces.

It was beautiful.

It was real.

I wondered what would happen if this became common practice, not just during mega-evangelical events, but every Sunday. What if during small group, this public confession became a part? What if in Lori's living room, we smashed our tea cups against the wall in anger at the injustice of what women experience? What if we sang aloud our own secret transgressions and held each other as the guilt shattered like glass?

"Hello, I'm Caroline and I'm a mess."

"Hi, Caroline."

What would it look like if instead of receiving the message of grace, we became it?

The small circles of college students I saw reminded me of every recovery meeting I've ever been to in church basements or middle school gyms or outside huddled in 20°F weather in cyclones of vape smoke or in front of a screen with my ear buds in during global pandemics when I'm afraid to leave the house. In the Bible, the Apostle James says to confess our sins to one another so that we might be healed.[75] This passage of scripture is one of the foundations of recovery.

Another pillar that is braided within it? We are called to do this confessing in community.

Churches like to tout *in community* on their bulletins and blogs and websites for good reason. Out of all the tools that God has provided me to heal, there is none more effective, in my opinion, than fellowship. One of the things that makes addiction so destructive is the way that it isolates and keeps us from connecting with others. That crouching lion is continually lying-in wait.[76] But when we're in the powerful presence of others? We have support and reinforcements against an attack.

To add kindling to the fire of addiction, trauma creates so much fear around connection, intimacy, and vulnerability that it further isolates (my own experience has been pushing all the right ones away and letting all the wrong ones in). Trauma is scarily so prevalent in women with addiction issues, it's no surprise the layers of shame and guilt and unworthiness work together to further separate people like me from connection with others, the church, and God. We are all standing behind the weight of our secret walls.

We cannot have community without honesty. Here I'm going to dig back into scripture again. Why? Well because there's some (or a lot) of truth there. As I've mentioned, I'm no Bible scholar and didn't grow up in the church and my dad is the furthest thing from a preacher (he's a psychologist). But I've read scripture and I've read it in community with other women and it speaks to me something living and active and true. It offers a beautiful story—one that I can feel my own story in.

Again, James states that when we confess our sins to each other we may be healed. I remember the first time I read this verse, something clicked. In my own experience, when I finally opened up and started trusting people enough to share, the more I talked about my past with others, the easier it became until it was almost second nature. Now, I have to hold myself back from telling the grocery store clerk about my character defects and dysfunctional past.

Just a side note, but I'd like to point out that James says "may be." Not, "will be."

Therefore, confess your sins to each other and pray for each other so that you may be healed.[77]

We already know this from the Apostle Paul's life that sometimes you ask for God to remove things (thorns, for example) and He just won't. God knows why certain prayers are answered and certain ones are not answered the way we would like them to be. Like why sometimes people make it out alive like me, and others—like Alex and Karissa—do not. Paul begged for his thorn to be removed three times, but the Lord said no. For Paul, as with all of us, Christ's power is made perfect in weakness; for God to be revealed in Paul's life, Paul had to continue to struggle with this thorn. Paul says: "Therefore, I will boast all the more gladly about my weaknesses, so that Christ's power may rest on me. That is why, for Christ's sake, I delight in weaknesses, insults, in hardships, in persecutions, in difficulties. For when I am weak, then I am strong."[78]

Because of Jesus's response that grace is sufficient for Paul, that his power would be made whole in Paul's weakness and brokenness, Paul says what the heck—then let's celebrate and boast! Let's be glad in these weaknesses. Let's shout. Let's shatter. Let's dance.

So, how do we "boast in our weaknesses?"

We share them.

When I think about who I have confessed my dark things to, I'd like to note here that they are always people I trust; always people I've been in relationship with. Not the church ladies who never talk about their dirt (sorry ladies, I have an affinity for the grass-stained Jesus groupies) or the co-workers who spend too much time gossiping and taking two-hour mani-pedi lunch breaks. No, I'm talking about the real deal: women who I trust and who have shared with me some of their dirt. First.

One of the many things I love about recovery is that we are a rag-tag bunch that don't generally have much to lose when we share about our lives: what we have come through, the messes we've caused and the relational dysfunction we've sown. You get what you get—and just when you think what you have done or not done is the worst thing any human being has ever participated in, someone shares with you that they are 1000% worse but also exactly like you. Exactly like me. And that's a relief.

Chapter 20:
CONSCIOUS CONTACT

Only essence speaks to desperate people.
— Anne Lamott

H aving experienced trauma and later being diagnosed with PTSD, my body was always on high alert. For years, my "world [was] experienced with a nervous system that [had] an altered perception of risk and safety."[79] A loud car engine goes by, someone drops a plate at a restaurant, a child cries out down the road: my brain tells my body to either shut down completely or run (enter kind old Mr. Anxiety Attack). It is not surprising, then, that I learned after years of struggling with mental health issues caused by trauma and addiction that it took nothing less than a supernatural intervention to heal me. My ways didn't work, even when I got into community and started to feel like a part of it; even after I opened my heart to the vulnerable act of sharing (or confession), it was clear that more was at work in my life that needed to be addressed. I needed to do more soul searching and more work to seek out the God who had been on my heels for some time.

I needed more of the good stuff.

Over the years, I've done quite a bit of "research" to try to come up with my own coping skills. Drinking (any amount or any kind of alcohol I wished), "controlled" drinking (only on weekends, only beer, only wine, only hard liquor that is healthy and clear, only after five o'clock, pot smoking (for medicinal purposes), dating (Mr. Wrong again and again, preferably in Wranglers)—these (for obvious reasons) never quite filled up the place that needed filling in my heart and soul. These coping strategies weren't only ineffective, they actually caused me more harm.

One of my earliest addiction treatment counselors said to me:

"Insanity is repeating the same behavior and expecting different results."

The result of my years-long research in active addiction and self-destruction was this: my ways don't work. Eventually, I turned to prayer because I saw my people in recovery do it and I felt the power of a conscious contact with God in my own life.

Trappist monk and theologian Thomas Merton wrote a sweet little ditty called *Seeds of Contemplation*. One of the benefits (maybe the only one) of being so scared to be vulnerable with others for so long is that I got in some good reading time. Merton states in the beginning of the book that it is primarily for monks, but that the tools in it can be applied more generally to any lay person of faith; you know, your everyday monk (or monkess) or former alcoholic or addict. As Merton (and first Brother Lawrence) called it, "practicing the presence of God," takes discipline; but it is completely accessible to everyone. I've heard sermons that mention this is what is meant by "praying continually" in the first letter to the Thessalonians.[80]

I started to wonder how I could even attempt this strange new concept of praying all the time and what this meant. Even in the bathroom? While doing the mundane things: washing dishes or walking the dog? Scrolling Instagram or Facebook? Step 11 of Alcoholics Anonymous states: "we sought through prayer and meditation to improve our conscious contact with God as we understood Him, praying only for knowledge of His will for us and the power to carry that out."

Easier said than done?

Does prayer really work?

I decided to do my research again and what I found was pretty amazing. Countless stories about prayers being answered.

Tara Geraghty, a mother from New Jersey, was devastated when her then three-year-old daughter Emily Grace began to breathe abnormally. She long knew something was not right with her baby but her medical tests did not reveal any underlying conditions. When she rushed Emily to the emergency room, the doctors told the mother they were surprised that the baby was still breathing. They added that her baby would have died if she had been admitted to the emergency on time. Hearing that, Tara told the medical experts that it must be a sign that God wasn't going to take her child away from her. Soon, Tara was informed that her child was diagnosed with stage 4 cancer. Tara and her family were heartbroken. She sat by her child for the next 78 days and prayed for the healing of her dear daughter.

"I prayed for her like I have never prayed before. She was on every prayer list you could imagine," said Tara, according to the *Readers Digest*. She believed in God, and her prayers were answered. Tara's daughter was healed completely, and the proud mother knows it was the doing of God.[81]

There were so many other stories of miraculous answered prayer that I found like one in *Reader's Digest* about Helene Casinelli Pileggi, a teacher from Pennsylvania.

When I was three-months-old, I developed spinal meningitis. I was given my last rites and was told I would not make it through the night. The prayer chain went out that night and my parents, who maintain a strong Catholic faith, never left my side. The morning came and the doctors we amazed by my progress. Even though I survived, my parents were told that it would be a long time to see what the prognosis may be for my quality of life. I was never supposed to talk or walk, and potentially have mental impairment. My parents and family kept their faith and by the "will of God," I survived and thrived throughout my childhood and into adulthood with minimal sicknesses.

Fast forward to five years ago. At the age of 34, I was diagnosed with stage two breast cancer. I am the first in my family to ever experience breast cancer. Once again, the prayer chain went out. I went through many treatments and was able to stay cancer free for four years. Then, this past spring of 2017, I was diagnosed with stage four breast cancer that metastasized to my lungs. It was one of the hardest times of my life. However, with my team of doctors and the amazing support of my family, friends, and faith, my cancer is shrinking and accepting my treatments.

I say the rosary every morning giving thanks for God's healing. I am a true believer in putting everything in "God's hands."[82]

I continued reading and learning and listening in recovery meetings. There were so many accounts here of prayers being answered (sometimes quickly, sometimes slowly), there aren't enough pages of books to recount them. I thought about what Lisa had asked me to do in writing a care-of-God list and how many times prayer was actually a part of those moments when God had come through. Even if just a silent witness. I recalled how often prayers begin and end recovery meetings, the central role it plays in my own church's worship service, and how believers over the ages have knelt, wept, face down, arms up, crying out, a heart-call to God. Together.

I can't give you a practical breakdown of "how-to" pray. I wish I could in a colorful Instagram carousel of graphics. Or perhaps a TikTok or Reel where I am dancing, doing jumping jacks and pointing to a bullet point list that appears magically with each well-timed signal. What I can share is a couple hints that I have learned or practiced over the years that has helped to increase—or even begin—building my faith and sustaining my recovery.

First, I suppose it makes sense to begin the way that Jesus asked us to pray in scripture. His teaching on prayer happens a couple times and I'll focus on his discussion in Luke 11: 1-13.

> *One day Jesus was praying in a certain place. When he finished, one of his disciples said to him, "Lord, teach us to pray, just as John taught his disciples."*
>
> *He said to them, "When you pray, say:*
>
> *'Father, hallowed be your name, your kingdom come. Give us each day our daily bread. Forgive us our sins, for we also forgive everyone who sins against us. And lead us not into temptation.'*
>
> *Then Jesus said to them, "Suppose you have a friend, and you go to him at midnight and say, 'Friend, lend me three loaves of bread; a friend of mine on a journey has come to me, and I have no food to offer him.' And suppose the one inside answers, 'Don't bother me. The door is already locked, and my children and I are in bed. I can't get up and give you anything.' I tell you, even though he will not get up and give you the bread because of friendship, yet because*

*of your shameless audacity he will surely get up and give
you as much as you need.*

*"So, I say to you: Ask and it will be given to you; seek and
you will find; knock and the door will be opened to you. For
everyone who asks receives; the one who seeks finds; and to
the one who knocks, the door will be opened.*

*"Which of you fathers, if your son asks for a fish, will give
him a snake instead? Or if he asks for an egg, will give him a
scorpion? If you then, though you are evil, know how to give
good gifts to your children, how much more will your Father
in heaven give the Holy Spirit to those who ask him!"*

In essence, Jesus says this: Ask me.

Early on my recovery journey, there were a couple recovery meetings I attended that ended with the Lord's prayer. Then there were
some with the Serenity Prayer[83] or the 3rd Step Prayer[84]. Always bookended by a moment of silence in the beginning for those still suffering
and a closing that helped me look upwards.

It was a bit later as I continued reading books by sober Christians
and other authors that I heard about a simple repetitive prayer, "Lord
Jesus Christ, have mercy on me." It is the hallmark of the classic *The
Pilgrim's Way,* written by an anonymous author that I like to imagine
was an old woman who disguised her female status like George Eliot
did when she wrote *Middlemarch* (for those of you who aren't book
nerds like me, forgive this allusion). Similarly, Brennan Manning sites
repetitive prayer as being helpful on his own journey as he struggled
with alcoholism. He wrote about several transformational moments in
his life that were bookended by what felt like an almost ecstatic prayer

experience after praying short, simple prayers like "Abba, I trust in you." And one of my all-time favorite prayers was talked about in a book by Anne Lamott and is the title of her book: *Help, Thanks, Wow.* Fairly sure my prayer life can be summed up nicely by these three words.

God knows what we need and created prayer or communication with Him as a healing act in and of itself, one that can promote self-regulation and balancing. Even Jesus, himself, frequently went to quiet places (or attempted to) to spend time in contemplation and connection with his Father.[85] I cite these examples in some books because I find it more than interesting that authors throughout the ages (and I could cite literally hundreds upon thousands and possibly millions of examples here) have noted how simple prayers can open up a connection to God that is healing and transformational. And it's not just something that happens in sanctuaries. Prayers, simple prayers, can connect anywhere.

After learning some of this I decided to give it a try. Especially Brennan Manning's example of simply saying, "Abba (or Daddy or Jesus), I trust in you." I loved the "shocking accessibility" of God in this word, *Abba.*

God may be the Sovereign of the Universe, but through his Son, God has made himself as approachable as any doting human father.[86]

I recall how ridiculous I felt as I made a meal, took a shower, and walked my dog, whispering in my mind the small, five words: "Abba, I trust in you." Had a tough day? "Abba, I trust in you." Tough hour? "Abba, I trust in you." I said the prayer. Conflict with family? "Abba, I trust in you." Confusion with what I saw on the news? "Abba, I trust in you." Prayer. Over a couple days, then weeks, I started noticing something. The more I said the prayer, the more connected to God I felt.

While I hoped to keep this up for a long while, this conscious repetition grounded in the centuries-old practice by hidden mystics didn't last as long as I wanted. It did, however, change me.

Eugene Peterson, the guy who translated the Bible for folks like me (*The Message*) wrote an interesting book called *A Long Obedience in the Same Direction*. In it, he discusses the walk of faith and all things it requires, like persistence as outlined in the pilgrim's psalms of ascent. The Psalms of Ascent are psalms 120-134 in the Old Testament that were sung by Jewish pilgrims during holy festivals as they journeyed up to Jerusalem. In the epilogue (note: please read epilogues), Peterson shares about the importance of reading scripture prayerfully.

When I first read this, what came to mind were the five words that clung to my heart like super glue as a new believer (Abba, I trust in you) and how prayer has changed my life. And then another question came to mind: is it possible to read scripture prayerfully? I wonder now, if this question was posed to me long before I read the Bible at all, what I would think or say.

I love the way Peterson sums it up:

Prayerfully. We are taught to read in order to gather information. Our schools train us to read books so that we can pass examinations. We're good at looking for facts. "Knowledge is power," they tell us. Books contain stuff that we can use to get a degree, fix an engine, hold down a job, solve a mystery. But the Bible is not primarily a source of information; it is one of the primary ways that God uses to *speak to us.* "God's Word" we call it, which is to say, God's voice—God speaking to us, inviting, promising, blessing, confronting, commanding, healing. The Bible is not so much God telling us some *thing*—some idea, some fact, some rule—as God speaking life into us. Are we listening? Are we answering?[87]

Have you heard the African proverb that says: "When you pray, move your feet?" For me, prayer doesn't have to be a sedentary thing. It can be carried along with me, when I'm reading the Bible, reading my newsfeed, or talking with you. And walking.

Little did I know when I started my hobby of walking in recovery, Jesus was walking with me and healing me with each step.[88] Hikes through sand dunes and young pine forests, quiet swaths of oaks and rows of corn fields and the savannahs of my childhood, and now into my thirties, the magnolia groves and clay-soiled ridges that smell of bears and sunset: all of this mindful movement has helped to bring a sense of presence into my life, something those who experienced trauma often struggle with.

Now, some of my most treasured prayer times are when I'm walking in the woods or on a beach or in the mountains. There is a ninth-century Irish monk, John Scotus Erigena, who wrote: "Christ wears 'two shoes' in the world: Scripture and nature. Both are necessary to understand the Lord, and at no stage can creation be a separation of things from God."

As I started talking to God more in my imperfect, simplistic, and often quite selfish way (usually veering from the simple petitions and going on and on about the things I wanted at the time, like a family and a sexy husband who preferably was a doctor who would condone my then-nicotine habit), He was there not only healing my past traumas, but also making a way in the desert that I could clumsily walk through. As I sought to improve my conscious contact with Him, more was revealed.

One of the first times I went for a prayer walk in early recovery I was in an arboretum, down a winding path (I can see it now) with little limestone pebbles and tree roots like spider webs that wove back and forth over the tawny ground. The smell of the first spring blooms and the warm feel of sun on my flannelled arms—and birds sang and called as if they, too, remembered me and were bidding: "Hello, welcome back."

The walk this day was a prolonged exhale, an "a-ha," a love letter to myself. From that day forward I spent countless hours on countless trails in the Midwest, with my trusty companion, Mo, who loved to chase Lake Michigan waves and sprint up sand dunes, and then with the loves of my life in the South (more on that later) surrounded by blue, hazy mountains and towering, spindly trees. There is something healing about being in nature. My body knew this instinctively. It wasn't until much later that I learned that there has actually been research done about this very fact: people with trauma histories can neurologically heal from spending time surrounded by green, breathing in fresh air. What lovely gifts God has given us to heal: community and confession and nature and prayer. And how great to combine all four.

Today, I can go back to those healing trails in my mind when the stress gets to be too much or when the world goes too far off the deep end (like now, in 2020 as I'm writing this—do I need to say more?). This mindful reminiscence is another way to bring my God back to mind in a way that is visceral and healing and fun, like stepping in rain puddles. Today, when I need a pause—which is often—I go back in my mind or find a trail or park near our home to get back to what it means to be truly alive and human. Back to how it was before concrete and powerlines, cell phones and social media. Just me and God.

Take a walk with me now:

I turn right and pull into our favorite park. Mo is breathing heavy in the back seat, his sweet puppy tongue sloshing against the half-open window, smelling the earthy pines and feeling the beach air as we get closer. I pull into the parking lot and am the only car there. I feel so small in this big lot as I step out and look up. A hawk circles overhead and cries out as if to say hello against the vast pale blue etched with white feather clouds.

I kick-off my flip flops and lace up my hiking shoes as Mo pulls hard on the leash. He is ready to go. He knows the way—we've done this a few hundred times before—and heads towards the trees, not towards the shelter, where it looks like we should go. We head to this little hidden break in the foliage. Only people who have been there before, not tourists with maps, know the way. This little trail, only a couple feet wide climbs gradually and then bends to reveal a gully in the dunes. The trees line its ridges and there is a quiet here like silence I have never known—maybe why I love it so much.

God speaks in that familiar whisper and birdsong. I breath in slow and stop and close my eyes, the warm sun tickling my face, the smell of earth and beautiful decay and also new life. I open them and see how the light dances on the ground and in the leaves, making lovely shadows everywhere; I feel as if I am dissolving into them. Gratitude overwhelms.

Here, I come to the point in the path that narrows again and climbs still gradually along a dune where tree branches line and roots cartwheel up and down. To the left and right people have carved their initials and names and dates into the gray skins of resting trees. They don't seem to mind. Years have passed and these scars have become a part of them. I trace my fingertips along the bark as I pass and circle to the left down a couple steps (who came out here to build these steps for us?) and continue on and back down this stretch of forest dunes. I love this stretch because it is as if the trees are all signaling to the water, the hushed stillness before the perpetual wave. And the singing, the rejoicing: the trees are clapping in praise.[89]

The path moves straight and to my left there is the most magnificent tree. I celebrate this tree with its five trunks reaching out like giant's fingers towards the sky (in the future, this same tree would be where I swing and laugh and joyfully gaze at my husband to-be). I am getting close and Mo feels it too. And then I see it: the sand steps that lead to the sky. I ascend and begin to hear gentle lapping, louder as I climb—up, up, up—then I reach where the sand meets the sky meets the water.

And there is peace.

Abba, I trust in you.

Chapter 21:
ARE WE THERE YET?

Storytelling always has been, and always will be,
one of humanity's greatest tools for survival.
– Rachel Held Evans

S hame is hiding in the dark. It is wondering about my place in the world and never feeling good enough to be taking up the space I am. Shame smells like cannabis smoke and the slippery sour of condom wrappers and leaves decaying in fall. Shame is the rock that you can't drop. The lie that you didn't want to tell. The story that never gets told. Shame takes. Steals. Whispers. Shame is sad and worn-out and hobbles along. Shame can't look you in the eye, but often forces you to look through a broken mirror.

Shame permeates the lives of many women—like me—who struggled to connect with a faith community (any community) because of a tattered past. As I've shared with you, I was knee-deep in addiction by the time I was a teenager. I'd experienced repeated sexual traumas and limped along using substances like drugs and alcohol to self-medicate and treat what I didn't know at the time was post-traumatic stress. By the time I came crawling to the cross, I was worn out. Defeated. Crushed. I clung to anything that could explain the pain—and Jesus did that well. I could relate to many of the ideas in scripture, like losing one's life to find it—because my life, it seemed, had disappeared long ago.

Despite the shame that kept me stuck like I was doing a backstroke in an ocean of tar, connection with a faith community did happen, though it was a painful and slow process.

I remember the feeling of soft relief in my therapist's office the day it happened. Her eyes sparkled like a glittering lake as she said: "You have post-traumatic stress disorder." At thirty-years-old in addiction recovery and after having trudged through an overwhelming amount of the muck and pain of life, I was not prepared to be surprised. Or relieved. But I was both.

Everything made sense in retrospect, like a game of chess (shout out to *The Queen's Gambit* fans). She explained to me some of the symptoms (things I had experienced for years) and each word was like an embrace. All at once, it was as if the distorted notions that had plagued me for years like "I'm crazy" or "Something is wrong with me" had permission to retreat. Checkmate.

Since that day, many of the lies I've believed about myself, lies that led me down torturous roads of sexual violence and deep insecurity, have transformed over time into a more grace-filled and compassionate understanding of myself—a truer understanding of my identity. This didn't happen overnight or with idealistic finality, but the foundation was laid—or better, uncovered.

Trauma shows itself in a variety of ways. Some people with PTSD are tormented by a heightened sense of fear and exaggerated startle response (jumping out of my seat when I hear a loud noise, for example). Some experience anxiety, panic, depression, flashbacks, and disorienting disassociation like western Michigan snow storms. Some, like me, can only make sense of it all once it is named. For years (especially at the height of my addiction in high school) I was blinded by my symptoms. I couldn't see two feet in front of me. The world and everyone in it was moving in slow, excruciating motion.

Dr. van der Kolk, who wrote a foundational work on trauma called *The Body Keeps the Score,* asserts that "as long as trauma is not resolved, the stress hormones that the body secretes to protect itself keep circulating, and the defensive movements and emotional responses keep getting replayed." [90] It's no wonder that so many people, like me, turn to unhealthy coping mechanisms to ease this suffering, one of the most popular being substance use that often leads to a deep-rooted, snarling addiction.

After getting baptized and attending church in recovery, one thing that used to terrify me was going to church services. I dreaded the initial step of walking into the building. My hands tingling. My feet heavy as if walking under water. Figuring out where to sit was even more anxiety provoking. Strangers so close I could smell their aftershave. Or the violating glances and objectification. Sin can flourish in the sanctuary.

Not being able to control my immediate environment or being objectified in a presumed "safe space" made attending a regular church near impossible. Yet while trauma impacted my ability to truly connect with a faith community at that time, this was not the end of my story. Nor was it the full story. In fact, I would learn that Jesus, himself, declares victory over all of the mess that trauma can conjure in John 16:33: "In this world you will have trouble. But take heart! I have overcome the world."

In Psalm 147:3, the psalmist proclaims that "God is close to the brokenhearted and binds up their wounds." I have experienced the healing salve and seen with my own eyes the wounds of trauma disappear into wholeness. I have also learned that my difficulty in connecting with a faith community has been about more than just the physical space of the sanctuary. God has revealed that is has also been about the space or condition of my heart. And the hearts of others in the pews. As Christ followers, we are called to bind up the wounds of others—not looking the other way, but tending to and walking alongside those who suffer. Just like my therapist, my recovery family, and so many of my sisters and brothers in Christ, have done for me.

We can be a recovery community and faith community that learns, listens, and responds. We can be there when doors are opened to new and important conversations about our loving God and how He is there in times of hardship and trauma. We can be there when someone uses their voice and agency for the first time and we can be there when someone cries out to God and needs a shoulder to balance against. Jesus calls us to love our neighbors and this is a part of that honorable and challenging calling. My hope is that the recovery community and church (and maybe that means you) considers how these spaces can be welcoming for all people, including those who have trauma histories and related mental health concerns; how we can be a family with truly safe and open arms.

I have experienced this firsthand: God "sets the lonely in families, He leads forth the prisoners with singing."[91] So, how can we sing with each other and open up a space for listening, community, confession and prayer?

Even though addiction and trauma usually do need to be supported by a mental health professional, I'd like to invite us all to think about how more faith communities (this includes the recovery community) and churches and Christian leaders can be involved in encouraging individuals or families who are dealing with these issues. There are a number of ways to do this—and because research says that we all love our lists (shout out to all my blogger friends!), here's a list of five possible ways we can all step up.

1. **Create Opportunities for Safety**
   In many communities, the term "safe space" no longer feels safe. I someone tells asserts that a space is safe, that doesn't mean it is. Oftentimes, I have no reason to believe them other than that they told me (and for many of us, words only carry so much truth). They're going to have to prove it. Instead of declaring a space safe, what if faith communities thought about ways to provide opportunities for safety that someone can choose from? For example, what if there were male and female greeters on Sundays that offered to step aside with someone who is new and introduce them to someone they can sit by, or grab a cup of coffee with them before the service, or even just sit outside during worship and talk in order to feel a bit more comfortable?

2. **Determine if more Issue-specific Ministries are Needed**
   Most churches have issue-specific ministries. For example, a women's or men's ministry often provides gender-specific opportunities for fellowship, study, and engagement. What if more specific offerings could be explored? One idea for faith communities is to try to solicit volunteers and leaders and open small groups or other sharing circles around particular topics. These can include addiction, veteran's support, women's trauma support or others that people might be interested in. Our church recently started an evening Bible study for people impacted by PTSD that is led by a retired combat veteran.

This may be challenging with many congregations stretched thin, but with many more virtual opportunities now becoming available, it might be a great way to try something new.

3. **Gender or Issue-specific Events or Gatherings**

Along with exploring the possibility of issue-specific ministries or small groups, one-time or annual events can be explored as well. For women, there is a world-wide virtual and in-person event called *IF: Gathering* (I'll get to this in a minute). This gender-specific event focuses on issues specific to women and often touches on the more complicated aspects of the Christian walk and discipleship. I've also started the annual Women's Global Recovery Roundtable on International Women's Day, a time for women in addiction and mental health recovery and allies to join together and shine a light on women's issues. Additionally, faith communities can explore inviting outside speakers who bring a powerful personal testimony and wisdom around a particular topic so they can be more informed about the issues surrounding them in the community.

4. **Learn more about Trauma-informed Churches**

There are many resources on how to become more trauma-informed and create opportunities for safety that will feel welcoming and supportive. *Trauma Informed Churches* is a nonprofit organization whose mission is to provide practical ways the church can support individuals and families with trauma histories. On their website, there are ways to support trauma and related concerns like anxiety, depression, aggression, self-harming/self-loathing, withdrawal, eating disorders and sleep problems.[92]

5. **Have Recovery Coaches on Staff**

   Recovery coaches or peer support professionals are people who've experienced   addiction and/or mental health recovery and can uniquely speak to the needs of people struggling with their own recovery. They can also help others figure out if recovery is for them. Many churches across the country are exploring how to work with people in recovery to support those struggling.

The State of Tennessee, where I live now (hey y'all!), has a unique model of support funded through the Department of Mental Health and Substance Abuse Services called the Faith-based Initiative.[93] This statewide program was created in response to the opioid crisis. Leaders in the health department found an innovative way to leverage the incredible asset of support in faith communities, almost 12,000 congregations across the state with 85% of the population attending at least one of them regularly.[94] The Faith-based Initiative provides free training, certifies congregations so that they are "recovery-friendly," and employees people in recovery as a network of peer support throughout the overwhelmingly rural counties.

As Jesus said, "…if you have faith as small as a mustard seed, you can say to this mountain, 'Move from here to there,' and it will move. Nothing will be impossible for you."[95]

In our broken world, a world that is suffering and hurting on a larger scale every day, it is imperative that we learn how to bridge the gap between addiction and mental health recovery and faith.

Susan Battah-Horn, a recovery advocate in Florida says:

"We have a voice that needs to be heard. We are not mistakes. We do recover. We go from mess to messenger from test to testimony."

The Bible is clear: the mountain of addiction can be moved. There are countless ways that we can become the message, not just preach it.

We can bring the grace and vulnerability of the downstairs church to the pews upstairs. We can bring the treasures hidden in the off-pitch choir and gleaned from the sinful (like all of us) preacher and felt with the outrageous walk-on music entrances of lady Bible teachers. We can level the building.

Chapter 22:
THERE IS POWER

I am not free while any woman is unfree, even when her shackles are very different from my own.
— Audre Lorde

On long road trips to visit family in the Midwest, our family hurtles down the highway in our silver minivan (yes, I am now one of those women) and when we get to some of the larger cities we pass through like Indianapolis, Cincinnati or Chicago, I love to peer at the passing cityscape: the way cement dances and swirls into exits and turn lanes, this big crescendo of life and movement leading to a downtown in the distance with its looming skyscrapers and busyness. There is something very fascinating to me about how life moves. I love to watch my kids, too, as they peer with me and wonder or ask simple questions or provide the funniest commentaries on things like purple horses, school buses called Mrs. Fritter, and spiders who may or may not be afraid of thunder clouds.

There is a lot that goes on as we travel through towns and cities and catapult through time and space in our little box made of glass and metal. On these drives, I've had a lot of time to think about everything from my to-do lists to what book I want to read next to the memories in this book to stories in scripture that I've read or sermons I've heard over the years. One of the things that I've spent considerable time thinking about is the road to Damascus. What it looked like, what it smelled like (probably not pleasant), how the sunsets or sunrises reached above the shelves of golden rock, dirt, and dust in the distance.

What's amazing—downright ridiculous—to me is how anyone can walk this conversion road. It doesn't matter if we've had drug overdoses, given birth in prison, been assaulted, lost our spouse after decades or even just gone years without a pedicure—whether we think we deserve to walk it or not, we can. No matter what we've done or where we have come through, there is an awesome—yes AWEsome—promise from God that He will meet us where we are and love us no matter our wounds. The Apostle Paul's miraculous conversion on his way to the city of Damascus (outlined in the book of Acts) is something that many see as one of the most important events in all of scripture, because if someone like Paul can be converted and saved, anyone can.

Paul used to be called Saul and he was a horrific dude. He was a Jewish Pharisee, or teacher of the law, and spent most of his time persecuting Christians. Yes, that's right. Before he entered the scene as a Christian rockstar (think Jeremy Camp), he was more like Hannibal Lecter, figuratively speaking. The reason he was going to Damascus was to arrest Jewish Christians and bring them back to Jerusalem for trial and possibly execution. If Jesus could have an archenemy during this time in history, it would be Saul.

This is where things get interesting. On Saul's way to Damascus during the scorching heat of the desert day, "a light from heaven" shines down and he hears a booming voice from the clouds. Everyone traveling with Saul sees the light, but Saul sees the Lord himself. Saul is completely overwhelmed and falls to the ground. The voice thunders, making the ground beneath his feet tremble:

Saul, Saul, why do you persecute me?[96]

All at once, everything Saul had ever believed crashed down around him like rubble after an earthquake. He was a zealous Jew, thinking he had been doing right by God, but in reality, he was working against Him. His wretched life and his choices had kept him separated from the God he wanted to live for and he didn't even know it.

After the vision, Saul tried to get up from where he had been struck down and discovered that he was blind. The vision of the Lord and the power of this experience took his sight. Some scholars even speculate that he was hit by lightning. However it happened, he was so distraught after the encounter—and blind—that he had to be led into the city. Saul, the mighty and feared Jewish zealot, could no longer walk by himself. After he arrived in Damascus, he fasted for three days, struck by grief or penance. His blindness was a physical blindness, but also symbolizes a lack of spiritual vision. What happened on the road to Damascus helped Saul to see this.

What happens next is even more interesting. There is another man named Ananias who was a disciple of Jesus, and just as Saul was getting thrown from his horse and experiencing this amazing transformation, Ananias (miles away) heard the Lord call to him in a vision. God told Ananias:

Go to the house of Judas on Straight Street and ask for a man from Tarsus named Saul, for he is praying. In a vision he has seen a man named Ananias come and place his hands on him to restore his sight.[97]

Ananias was terrified because he heard about Saul and all of the horrible things he had done. As is God's fashion in his upside-down kingdom, God responds that he has been persistent in pursuing Saul, despite his actions and sins. God would use him in incredible ways, and most importantly, would continue (yes, *continue*) loving him. God said to Ananias later in Acts 9:15-16:

> *Go! This man is my chosen instrument to proclaim my name to the Gentiles and their kinds and to the people of Israel. I will show him how much he must suffer for my name.*

Talk about grace juice. This is the best of the best right here. Someone who was on his way to persecute Christians, God was going to use for His good and loving purposes? And to proclaim to the Gentiles!?! Note that the Gentiles were seen to be some of the lowest of the low, not the holier-than-thou, play-by-the-rules (or in the case, the Torah) Jews. Classic God. Turing the world upside down. Rescuing the broken. Being ridiculously persistent in love.

It wasn't all going to be easy or merry after Saul turned to God—or better, was catapulted towards God—and rescued his broken life. Nevertheless, God was saving him in real time, at the opportune moment, and he needed Ananias to help.

Paul's conversion is a Hollywood-esque style portrayal of God's incredible intervention in the broken life of a man who needed saving (just in case anyone is wondering, Bradley Cooper as Saul). One scholar notes that what can be applied to all stories of salvation and conversion like this one is "a personal encounter with Jesus Christ via a witness to the gospel, a response of surrender in penitence faith, and the reception of salvation blessing and incorporation into the church."[98] This sounds a little academic, but I like it. Basically, (1) encounter Jesus (with or without a bolt of lightning), (2) feel bad about what you've done/how you've lived (i.e., repent or turn in heart and action), (3) receive God's love and salvation (cool!), and (4) become a part of the family (my advice: bring a dish to your first church potluck).

After his conversion, getting a new name was probably the simplest thing to have to happen (the name change is mentioned later when he is in Cyprus in Acts 13:9). Saul/Paul has to work very hard to be accepted into a church he once shunned and actively tried to destroy. Understandably, it took the other believers time to trust that he was one of them. But once he opened his mouth and started preaching, it was hard for anyone to deny. Paul had a powerful encounter with God.

One thing they never tell you: the closer you get to thirty, the more it feels like either something amazing or something terrible is about to happen. Perhaps that is a side effect of crow's feet. Or Botox. For me, a worst-case-scenario contemplator (as my husband now calls me), those two large numbers—3-0—loomed eerily. It was back then, when I was two years sober and not yet feeling pressured to weigh the advantages of medical spas, that I had one of those weeks. It's funny how this happens: when you need to learn something (even if for the hundredth time), it's coming at you from a thousand different directions like lake effect snow. If you've lived in western Michigan, you know what I'm talking about.

First, on Sunday my church hosted visiting missionaries that talked about their travels with tan, worn faces and jubilant eyes. They stood in front of our congregation and told stories about learning a strange language and becoming family with people who were eager to learn more about a God they didn't know yet. I shifted in my seat and looked around. Most eyes in the room were on them or flitting back and forth to squirrely kids coloring on programs or looking at iPads. Then on Tuesday, someone suggested I read a book about an ocean-eyed woman who worked in children's ministry. I thought I was too busy, so instead flipped through its pages and brushed my hand against the black and white images of little humans who looked like joy personified: all smiles and eyes. I could almost hear their laughter. Next, I happened upon a website during mindless scrolling on a Thursday that talked about how planting gardens where empty city space used to be brought glory to God. On the website, there were a lot of hip-looking millennials with skinny jeans and dreadlocks and contoured makeup and long necklaces with their hands raised and eyes closed. They made faith look really cool, like dirty hair with just the right amount of dry shampoo.

And then finally on a Friday, after wondering what I was supposed to be learning from all of this, and feeling what I now refer to as the "God Nudge," I found myself sitting around a circular table in a room mellow with faux firelight. Across from me was a middle-aged woman who looked so sure of herself, so secure in her own skin. Her outfit was more than a few years outdated, her hair looked like it was styled by Medusa, and she had a lipstick stain on her right front tooth when she smiled.

She was disheveled from battling rush hour traffic or perhaps a long day at work, but she had the most peaceful smile on her face. She reminded me of my friend Carolyn from Michigan, though Carolyn came from an era where you didn't leave the house without an ironed blouse. This woman was a mess on the outside, but had something bright on the inside—something I wanted.

Carolyn often told me about how she and her husband, who was an orthopedic surgeon, traveled to a city in Kenya each year. While he performed free consults and surgeries for people with broken bones and sore knees and elbows, she visited women who were lined up outside the building and down the winding road waiting to get help. She talked about praying with women who lost children; women who were raped by opposing armies; women who saw all the young men of their villages slaughtered in war. She told me of their faith. Despite their circumstances, these women told stories of healing and redemption with glittering eyes. They were people who had to learn how to grow around the pain and trauma, yet their faith shook the ground beneath them.

When Carolyn spoke, I drank in the stories she told of what the Lord can do when we believe with ferocity. Her own faith was infectious and solid. By nature, on the other hand, I am a skeptic. I don't believe anything to be true unless I see it with my own eyes. This is why when I first heard about some of these miraculous healings and happenings, even though I wanted them to be true with my whole heart, I said to myself, "Yeah, right." Maybe during the time of the Apostle Paul on the dusty road to Damascus or when Moses parted the Red Sea. Not today, not in the same era as Snapchat and Space Force and the Kardashians.

But over the years, I've heard story after story about how someone encounters Jesus and their life is rocked to its very core, whether through the laying on of hands or during long, fiery hours of worship in a building with dirt floors and no walls. Or in the hushed circle of a recovery meeting. People are healed and sight is regained—like the New Testament is shaken awake and breathing in the streets.

I've heard about God showing up in the most unsuspecting of places and through the most unsuspecting of people. Over the years, I've heard the stories of His persistent and ridiculous love in the downstairs church.

All of these things came to mind like light that breaking across a stormy sky the week I found myself at our church's IF: Gathering. It was my first time, and the way they kept talking about it during announcements and in the edgy, chic promo video—I had to give it a try. I am a sucker for FOMO (fear of missing out). And of course, Jennie Allen, one of the founders, is very disarming and has that Reese Witherspoon vibe, like every woman's best and better-dressed friend.

She and other women from diverse backgrounds and experiences bring truth and sling hope through this virtual conference that can be live streamed anywhere in the world at local churches or in living rooms.

The first night it was live streamed at our church was a Friday, and I was exhausted from work and graduate school and honestly was not in the mood to socialize, especially not with "church ladies." While the older lady across from me looked peaceful and had a certain something that I wanted (although I didn't know what that was), I didn't really want to talk to her. At two years sober, I was still pretty unsure about the church. I drank the blood and ate the body from the outside looking in. Friendly smiles and awkward handshakes during the brief two minutes the pastor gave for extending the peace or saying hi to our neighbors (I learned that it's explained in different ways in different spaces), but no real connection. No gritty vulnerability.

I had questions. Doubts. Insecurities. Fears (that I suspected these people knew nothing about). I was afraid if I got doused with holy water I might combust. Was my past too much for them? If they really knew me, would they smile as I walked in the front doors and hand me a program like everyone else or would they bolt the door shut?

If Christianity was the team, it felt like I was the last one picked. But I still kept showing up.

I took a deep breath.

Then another.

And another.

Maybe I am supposed to be here, I thought.

I instantly felt a little calmer. Breathing can help me do this. Sometimes reminding myself to breathe can bring me back to the present moment (without sounding too much like a mindfulness enthusiast, though I am one). There were lots of cozy sweaters and pretty cups of tea and warm coffee and table decorations that were arranged by the type of women who have an eye for flowery décor. I respect these ladies so much because this most definitely is not my spiritual gift. Then there was some teaching that followed that I don't remember too well (just being real) and then the worship portion began.

Once the music started, I remember feeling this growing sense of connection with the women in the room and the women across the world who were meeting virtually—we had brief glimpses of living rooms and church sanctuaries with hordes of women cheering and sipping their tea and coffee with piercings or pink lips and wearing their sweaters or tanks, whatever the weather of their country required.

I looked around the warm-lit room and the "church ladies" started to look more like me if I squinted my eyes. I felt a sense of connection. They looked like my mother and sister. I looked around some more and they looked like the woman down the block chasing her kids and trying to muster the strength not to holler; the woman in the line at the grocery store; the woman at the homeless shelter who was afraid for her children; they looked like the ragamuffins at the AA meeting: my people.

And then the music—

As you now know, I did not grow up in the church and wasn't baptized until I was in college. I had never heard songs like "Come Thou Fount" and "How Great Thou Art" until I was well into my twenties and I had no idea who Hillsong or MercyMe was. By the time I was twenty-two, I knew Jesus (had met him in a lily dress), but he felt far-away like that distant relative you don't know super well, who comes to holiday gatherings and is polite enough but you never really know what to say around them. Jesus was my Great Aunt Melba.

All at once the music started and something in my body said move. The beat was infectious; I generally don't have much rhythm and I thank my momma for that, but it was as if my body took over and had a mind of its own.

The very talented artist, Tasha Cobbs Leonard, began to belt it out:

"There is power in the name of Jesus."[99]

My body started to tremble.

I became self-conscious, like when you are in church and you're super concerned with how your voice sounds singing the latest trendy worship song. I was afraid that I was going to start convulsing uncontrollably and people would start thinking I was possessed, bring me some snakes to test me or expect me to start speaking in tongues (this is also not my spiritual gift). But this feeling of worrying about what people think vanished, thankfully, and as the music continued and repeated and looped—*there is power in the name of Jesus*—I suddenly felt God there. As my body swayed and shook, I felt an embrace—and, in my mind, the addiction, the traumas, the griefs, all of the big and little sorrows—I felt these chains breaking and falling to the floor around me. *To break every chain, break every chain, break every chain.*

He was close.

No longer like a distant relative and more like my close friend from childhood who I was seeing for the first time in a long time. There was instant familiarity. I knew Him and there He was, unlocking and dismantling my chains one by one. He was speaking truth to me and the truth I heard that night was: I no longer have to live in shame or darkness. And what's more—I was not alone. There were women all over the globe who were shaking and swaying and feeling those heavy chains fall to the floor with a clang. There were women like me who didn't grow up in the church or even feel comfortable there—yet—but were healing and finding faith in the grit of recovery.

Tears started to fall as the song ended. I looked around the room and had the sense that I was not the only one who experienced for the first time (but not the last time) such a tremendous, ridiculous belovedness. Despite church, I found Him there.

That night at the IF: Gathering, I also felt for the first time (but not the last time) that I was somehow mysteriously sharing in the sufferings of Christ, not alone, but with the thousands of other women across the world who were singing along with Ms. Cobbs. We have been broken down and imprisoned by our experiences of trauma and addiction and sexual violence and all of the things and yet, with God's help, we overcome. Love continues to triumph. No matter what, Jesus is there.

And maybe I did belong after all. Maybe what I found in the downstairs church of the recovery community, this vulnerable and real and miraculous healing, could be found upstairs, too.

This year, Tanya, the woman who gave birth to her baby in prison, is celebrating six years in recovery. She works for a nonprofit that distributes Naloxone to people who have just overdosed on opiates or heroin. Naloxone, or Narcan, is a life-saving medication that can revive people who have gone into respiratory distress after an overdose. She is also a counselor and peer support provider, someone who works with other women who are searching for a new way to live and for something to believe in. Her baby girl is now in elementary school and has bright, smiling blue eyes and blonde satin hair.

I recently asked Tanya when she realized that she was worth saving. Her eyes welled with tears—I could hear it over the phone. She paused and then said:

"It's a moment-by-moment, breath-by-breath journey."

I have seen with my own eyes the power of God working in people's lives, broken people like Tanya and me. I have witnessed His relentless love and experienced an unspeakable and magnificent glory—something that at one time in my life I didn't think I deserved. And love—this has been spoken to me through the most unlikely of people. Over the years I have learned more about the God of love through them, and more about the truth of who I am. The dusty road to Damascus might be a freeway today, one that looks like a giant cement octopus from the sky, but it can still be trudged with red-painted toenails, and worn, blistered feet.

Miracles do happen. Maybe not in the same, big way; maybe not remembered for millennia. But ours are here: every day and ordinary marvels that point to something larger, much larger, than ourselves. Anne Lamott says that "the miracle is that we are here, that no matter how undone we've been the night before, we wake up every morning and are still here. It is phenomenal just to be." God meets us, forever and always, no matter the messes we have made of our lives and no matter our chains. Even if we end up meeting Him among a small rag-tag bunch of alcoholics and addicts in a damp room underground.

My faith journey, as I've outlined in tidbits throughout this book (thanks for sticking with it!), has had its own dusty moments. It didn't happen like Saul-turned-Paul but I did get knocked off my own horse, so to speak. More times than I can count. And there may or may not have been lightning (I'll keep some things to myself). The person I used to be—someone who had to escape the pain, someone who couldn't live her values, someone who couldn't say no or yes at the times she really wanted to, someone who lived in painful spiritual blindness, was rocked to the core. The many life experiences (some big and some small) and the many people in my life (some who were passersby and some who stuck around) all worked to turn my blindness into sight. And then, as if this wasn't enough: God shined a light so bright in my heart that I could not help but respond. I could not help but sway and shake and move to the music. I could not help but trust that there is power in the name of Jesus.

And I just had to tell you.

Chapter 23:
THE HEART OF THE MATTER

*The future for Christians depends on
how we master the art of giving grace.*
– Philip Yancey

My transformation has happened because of cheap coffee in Styrofoam cups, sipped while listening to shining vulnerability behind a podium. My healing has also been made possible by the women sitting in a sanctuary around circular tables with fake flowers slow dancing in the centers. Ultimately, my life in recovery is made possible by God himself, giving me sweet glimpses of an eternal message through women who are messy and imperfect and broken. With amazing grace, these spiritual experiences in recovery— and in church—shake me to the core of my being, turning my insides out and making the unlovely beautiful.

While all of this is true, and I'm so grateful it is, it took too long.

I'd like to now ask a question with you. Or maybe a couple questions. Could my experience have been any different if I connected with a community—and in particular, a faith community—early on in my recovery journey? If I was able to let more of the shame of my past go sooner or had people come around me who understood what I needed, would my story have been different? The stories of some of the women I've met and worked with, loved and lost—could the trajectories of our lives have changed? What could have broken through our cement hearts sooner?

While it's easier and more convenient to blame others, especially the church, I'm not going to do that today. Though I'd like to say something a bit bold and unpopular, something like I think the church is failing women in addiction and trauma recovery and has been for a very long time.

Sarah Bessey in *Jesus Feminist* says it this way: "We tend to think en masse or point fingers as a coping form of disassociation from our own culpability. But Jesus was clear on this: renewal in your world starts in your own heart and life (181)."

What I would like to say today is from the Psalms (and I've said it several times throughout this book):

God is close to the brokenhearted.[100]

And let me say this again.

God is close to the broken hearted.

If this really is true (which I believe that it is) and God is in the broken and dark and messy places, then why do so many Christians (myself included) not spend more time in those places with the brokenhearted? Why do we run away from these issues, focusing on the politically expedient or the trendy or the popular causes? Why do we stay insulated in our closed circles that smell like too many shades of the same perfume? If we really are "pro-life" does this life not also include those who are enslaved by addiction and trauma? Doesn't life include the gritty realities of addiction and the hundreds of thousands of women struggling today?

There are so many questions.

I have so many questions.

But instead of pointing fingers and shifting the blame and painting shame in the same color on a different canvas, I'd like to encourage us all, especially those like me who have worn shame like a heavy coat in summer, that hope and healing and support is possible. Whether we are in a church building or in an alleyway or behind the reception desk of a recovery community center, we can come together to dissolve the shame that is keeping too many of us trapped in silence. We don't have to wait for someone in a church pew or at a pulpit to do it. I believe that's up to all of us—those of us in addiction and trauma recovery downstairs and my brothers and sisters in the pew upstairs— to step out and learn from Jesus. Follow the way.

As a recovery community or community of faith or both (we're not really that different after all), let's show up today for those who are still suffering in the quiet, empty darkness of their shameful pasts. Let's call it out and name the injustice. Let's share our experiences, hand-in-hand. Let's sing our chorus: "me, too," so that hopefully, indeed miraculously, healing will arise and our light, together, will break forth like the dawn.[101]

As Elisabeth Elliot says, "Of one thing I am perfectly sure: God's story never ends with 'ashes.' My recovery community has taught me about the woman I want to be—have to be. Not some picture-perfect woman who does everything right and who has a past as stainless as her white blouse—no, I am real and authentically me, stains and all. I want to accept my past, live faithfully in the present and look with hope towards the future because 'amid the fragility of our lives, we have wonderful reason to hope.'"[102]

Recovery gives me an opportunity at more than a new life—it gives me the gift of a new identity, one I can wear humbly (on the good days) always in recognition of where I've come from and with hopeful expectation of where I am going. But I'm not a hero. My story is not another feel-good story about a woman overcoming adversity (although I have jumped over a few hurdles). The last thing I want you to say to yourself or your neighbor after reading this book is: "Wow! Caroline is inspiring! Amazing! [Fill in the blank] So cool!" Every human being on the planet has their own sufferings, their own traumas, and their own thorns. I fart just like you. What I do hope you take away from this is that my story is God's story. My story is a display of His splendor and a portrait of His persistence. A picture of how grace happens in the basement. My life as I've recounted it in little bits shows just what a small and clumsy clay jar I am and what a magnificent and all-surpassing power and glory is God. My life is a glimpse into how our Creator brings beauty from ashes and makes these ashes shine.

My story is also your story. And it joins with yours to make a pretty amazing picture. I've quoted Henri Nouwen a lot—because his story rings true for me—so here's another one:

> We all reflect God's love in different ways. Together we are like a mosaic. In a mosaic one stone is bright, another stone is gold, another stone is small. If we look at it closely, we can admire the beauty of each stone, but if we step back from it, we can see that all the little stones reveal a beautiful picture and tell a story that none of the stones can tell by itself. Together the different stones reflect the face of God to the world.[103]

All of my life experiences—the trauma and addiction and recovery and supporting other women—have led me to question the "whys," yet they have allowed me to rest firmly, solidly, in faith in a loving and more-than-powerful God. He is crazy in love with me. Each person at just the right time (Kairos) showed up for me. Those I worked with or felt called to help led me to a new place of healing and understanding and self-forgetting. Through the hands of some people, I had suffered some of the most horrendous things; yet through the eyes of others, I was offered healing. Recovery has shown me a picture of the humanity of Jesus with all its thorns and temptations and trials and grief—but also the marvelous parts, like love and tenderness and mercy.

Even Tanya—after six DUIs, a ruined career and marriage, expecting a baby girl in prison, and all the secret struggles she ran from—deserved a second, third, fourth, fifth, sixth, infinity chance. So do I.

And so do you.

If we are breathing, the door is there.

God says:

Hey! You over there! My sweet. You are beautiful. And I love you no matter what. You will get through all of this, I promise! And you know what? It's not just about getting through it—there are amazing things ahead, wonderful things that I have promised that you can hope for! I have given you a future; I will not harm you![104] And guess what? I will give you opportunities to love like you have been loved! Hold on, my sweet one. It's going to be unforgettable.

There is a picture of us during one of the annual Connections Counseling summer lake trips where counselors, mentors and patients met to grill out, hike, and enjoy the windy warmth of an August evening. The circle of flannel and denim and top-knots and thick eyeliner and piercings…how I loved and still do our rag-tag group of recovering alcoholics and addicts. Some of us sat pretty on our "pink clouds" as they call them in recovery: everything new and amazing with the promise of a better life, combined with our brains actually healing from the damage we caused, creating the perfect environment for hope. And then some of us were years in recovery, a little more grounded in the reality that the longer you don't put alcohol and drugs into your system, the more "life stuff" comes up that you actually have to deal with.

This picture was taken while we were all sitting in a circle after having gone around one-by-one to share something we were grateful for. For those who have never been to a recovery meeting of any kind, gratitude is something that comes up quite a bit. It's rare to be in a room filled with people who are only there because of second or third or fourth or an innumerable number of chances and not hear the words "thankful" and "grateful" and "gratitude."

The backdrop of the photo, with the lake and a setting sun and the director of the clinic, my good friend Shelly Dutch, standing off to one side. Such a beautiful picture of what we live every day in recovery. Shelly likes to say, "recovery is a we thing." If it were not for that circle of close friends and strangers, people that I could open my heart to, I would not be sitting here or writing this today. It was only in allowing someone else to hear my pain and help me carry it, and to help carry the burdens of others, that healing started to blossom. This is what saved me in recovery: the opportunity to be there for someone else.

I've found this to be true throughout my life, in recovery and before: the only time I feel true joy and true peace is when I am living for something or someone other than myself; when I let Christ in my heart enough to pour into my hands and out into the world. It is then that the mysterious and living Glory can make my life mean something for someone else. Brennan Manning was a priest and person in recovery who shared openly about his joys and struggles. He says that his own journey has taught him that "only when I feel safe with God do I feel safe with myself. To trust the Abba who ran to His wayward son and never asked any questions enables us to trust ourselves at the core."[105]

We must trust that we are a part of a new and better story, one where we get to share our testimony with others who are struggling, share about a God who loves us through our brokenness and the *horrible, beautiful process* of suffering,[106] and waits with open arms when we come running home. We get to tell our story by showing up for others who are looking for the same answer, the same *Someone* to love them; people who need to see, like I do, the unrelenting love of God. It doesn't matter if we do this in a church basement, a sanctuary, or along a coastal highway.

In the concluding pages of *What's So Amazing About Grace?* Philip Yancey notes:

> Sometimes as I went up and down the stairs connecting our church sanctuary to the basement, I thought of the upstairs/downstairs contrast between Sunday mornings and Tuesday evenings. Only a few of those who met on Tuesday evenings returned on Sundays. Though they appreciated the church's generosity in opening its basement to them, the AA members I talked with said they would not feel at ease in church. Upstairs people seemed to have it together, while they were just barely hanging on. They felt more comfortable in the swirl of blue smoke, slouched in metal chairs in jeans and a T-shirt, using swear words if they felt like it. That's

where they belonged, not in a stained-glass sanctuary with straight-backed pews.

If only they realized—if only the church could realize—that in some of the most important lessons of spirituality, members of the basement group were our masters. They began with radical honesty and ended with radical dependence. Athirst, they came as "jolly beggars" every week because AA was the one place that offered grace on tap.[107]

Recovery is a ray of sunshine. A bird song. An ocean wave and a white beach. Recovery is sticking my toes in the sand. It is taking a deep, full breath. It is grounding down, rolling my neck and shoulders. It is upward and then downward dog. It is a cup of tea on a cool day or a bowl of ice cream or strawberry salad on a summer afternoon. Recovery is also the smell of a wet dog that rolls around on a dead fish (true story—Mo!). A stubbed big toe or a weird ear. Recovery is an awkward conversation and a fender bender. It is a tough break up and a tear-stained fight. Recovery is your car breaking down in January and never making that phone call you need to make. Recovery is a stack of unpaid bills. Recovery means everything and nothing. Like this strange, lovely life, recovery is all the things at different times. It is one of the most difficult things I've ever done, yet at the same time it's so simple. And each of these things—doing the hard stuff and celebrating the most amazing joys and successes— is all a part of it. The bad and the good. The lovely and the unlovely. It is just like me. And you.

And it's just like the church: both grace-starved and grace-filled. Depending on the day (and some would argue, denomination).

What is most amazing, I've learned, is that recovery and faith— this long and winding road—is not about me at all. Those cairns and markers along the path, those people and experiences, have all led me to what I was searching for in my desperate addictions and unhealthy relationships: love and God. To learn that God's love for me and for all of us would persist no matter what. But this unending love wasn't just for me, not entirely. God's love has been freely given to me, graced to me, so that I would be able to put my own rock, my own life, on the pile and be a small piece of the way in someone else's journey. My life, dear friends, is for you.

You might be surprised to see me sitting next to you at church or in line at the coffee shop. You might not know I am sitting in the table next to yours at the restaurant or my child is sitting next to yours on the bus. You might not know that a part of my story may even be your story. Or perhaps you are the woman sitting next to the scared young girl in the hallway, called to be her second or seventh or infinite chance. Perhaps your own life is meant to reflect the image of a God you've been searching for your whole life.

Conclusion:

NOW WHAT? DO SOMETHING.

I f you are like me while reading a book, you might earmark pages
or make notes or highlight whole paragraphs if you connect with
something in it. It might even inspire you to do something. To
live your life a little different. To change. And if you are like me, this
usually doesn't last too long—unless, of course, you have someone to
hold you accountable to it. So, this is what I am proposing:

Take some time to sit with this book. Look over the questions
in Appendix A. Organize a book club or Bible study around some of
the topics discussed. Talk about it in your small groups and in your
college ministry and at your fancy women's teas. Then go out into the
world and find the woman who needs to know that God loves her—
truly, madly, deeply (don't you just love that song from Savage Garden
from 1997?). Here are a couple other ideas:

Learn about the recovery community organizations in your area
and donate money or time or other resources.

Share your own experience if you are in a person in recovery
(from anything) or just because you are a human being and have

lived experience that someone will connect with. Hope is a powerful thing.

Talk to your church about its addiction recovery ministry. If your church does not have one or is not connected to some type of recovery support service, pray about this and talk to people and try to discern if God is calling you and your church into this.

If you don't belong to a church or if you feel like you don't belong, talk to someone you trust about this. Talk about the whys.

Research recovery homes in your community or in your state and learn more about how they are helping your neighbors. If there isn't one in your community for women, talk to someone who might be interested in figuring out why and then do something about it.

Learn more about the recovery support services for youth, like recovery high schools, collegiate recovery programs, and alternative peer groups. How are college ministries connecting with these supports? Are there enough services for young people in recovery in your area? If there isn't, what can you do about it?

Trauma is a part of too many people's stories—and too often forgotten about when planning recovery support services, faith-based recovery programs and even church services. Check out the list of resources in Appendix B and educate yourself.

Go for a walk and pray.

Listen.

Tell me about how you've responded by visiting www.brightstoryshine.com and dropping me a message.

With hope,
Caroline

Appendix A:

STUDY GUIDE FOR SMALL GROUPS OR JUST YOUR LOVELY SELF

These questions are meant to help you or a small group read through this book with thoughtfulness and offer opportunities for reflection. I encourage you to grab a friend (or friends) and a journal, and journey with me through some gritty and real and beautiful things.

After each set of questions, I also encourage you to read and reflect on the scripture passages highlighted in each chapter and share any insights with your group or a trusted friend.

Prologue: Before You Begin
- What do you hope to get out of reading this book?
- Is there anyone who you'd like to invite on this journey with you?
- As you read, make note of certain passages of scripture referenced that speak to you and why.

Chapter 1

- Why do you think the author chose to begin the book with a story about Tanya?
- Put yourself in Tanya's shoes: how would you feel in this situation?

Chapter 2

- If you feel comfortable sharing: has anything happened in your own life that has changed how you feel about God or others?
- What role has fear played in this situation or experience?
- What are some times in your life (or in the lives of others) that you feel Jesus weeping?

Chapter 3

- How do you view people with an addiction or in addiction recovery? How do you view yourself?
- What do you think has helped to shape your views?

Chapter 4

- What were your twenties like? Or what are they like now? Do you struggle with any mental health challenges?
- Has anyone ever showed up unexpectedly to help you?

Chapter 5

- Why is there power in vulnerability?
- Is it difficult for you to be vulnerable or honest with others? Why or why not?

Chapter 6

- Have you ever been to a recovery meeting (AA, NA, another 12-step fellowship, Celebrate Recovery, SMART Recovery)? What was your experience like?
- Have you ever struggled with feeling like you are "enough?" What does this mean to you? What contributes to feeling like this (or not feeling like this)?

Chapter 7

*If done in a group setting, Question #1 might be challenging for some to share. It is recommended that for personal reflection only, unless there is a mental health professional facilitating the group.

- Sexual violence and trauma can be a difficult topic for many. If you are a survivor of sexual violence, do you have the support you need? Have you addressed this trauma in your life?
- Are you aware of the issue of human trafficking in your community?
- How do you think addiction, trauma, and trafficking are related?

Chapter 8

- Have you ever told your recovery or another life story? If so, how did this feel? What did you learn from the experience?
- Did you learn something new about addiction in this chapter? If so, what did you learn? How did this challenge your preconceived notions about addiction?

Chapter 9

- Has there been anyone in your life who has reflected the love of God back to you so that you learned more about

Jesus? If yes, who? Have you ever been this person for someone else? Explain.

- How do you reconcile faith with experiences of struggle or pain? If you cannot, what can you do to look into this issue further?
- What is the concept of "Kairos" explained in this chapter? How might you think about this as it relates to your own recovery or faith journey?

Chapter 10

- Has there been anything about your life or things you have experienced that have gotten in the way of your relationship with God and/or church? Share if you feel comfortable.
- Have you ever been a part of a small group at a church? If so, what was (or what is) this experience like? How is it similar or dissimilar to recovery meetings?

Chapter 11

- Do you know someone who has experienced an overdose or perhaps lost a family member or child to addiction? How has this experience affected them and/or you?
- What are some of the ways volunteer work or service has been important to you? Has working with others changed you or taught you anything?

Chapter 12

- Read this verse from Romans 8:28:
  And we know that in all things God works for the good of those who love him, who have been called according to his purpose.
- What does this verse bring to mind? What emotions, thoughts or memories come up for you?

Chapter 13

- What is your "healing forest" like? Or do you need to create/find one?
- Are there patterns in your life that keep you stuck? How do you address them?

Chapter 14

- What does the book of Ruth teach us about God?
- Have you ever had an experience with a female friend or group of women that taught you something new about yourself and/or God?

Chapter 15

- Read the excerpt (aloud) that the author reads in community with other women at a church event.
- What comes up for you?

Chapter 16

- Have you ever danced sober? What was this experience like?
- How do you talk about addiction? Did you know that how we talk about it can eliminate or perpetuate stigma? What does this mean to you?

Chapter 17

- How have relationships with other women shaped or changed you?
- Would you like to work on being intentional about putting energy into your female relationships?

Chapter 18

- What comes to mind when you hear the word "Christian?"

- Write your own "Care-of-God" list. Include all of those moments where you know God was there, where you experienced His presence or when you knew He was there during a difficult or joyful time.

Chapter 19

- Read this passage from the book of James 5:16:
  Therefore, confess your sins to each other and pray for each other so that you may be healed. The prayer of a righteous person is powerful and effective.
- How do you feel about the concept of "confession?" How does this relate to vulnerability?

Chapter 20

- Do you practice prayer? If so, what does your prayer life or habit look like?
- If you don't pray, why not? What are some other ways that you cope with life or work on your recovery?
- Do you read the Bible? Why or why not?

Chapter 21

- The author talks about how shame has worked against her in her own life and kept her isolated from both a recovery and faith family. Are there things in your life that are keeping you away from others? Would you like to change that?

Chapter 22

- What do you think of the conversion story of Saul of Tarsus?
- Have you ever had a conversion experience?

Chapter 23

- What are some ways that the faith and recovery community can support one another?
- What does the concept of radical grace mean to you?

Chapter 24

- How has your concept of addiction, mental health or trauma recovery changed since reading this book?
- How can community transform our individual struggles and collective experience of issues like addiction and trauma?

Conclusion

- Share with the group one or more scripture passages that were referenced in the book and why they stuck out to you.
- Do you feel called to action after reading this book? If so, how?
- Share with the group how you will respond to any calls or God-nudges you receive after reading this book.

Appendix B:
ADDITIONAL RESOURCES

Bright Story Shine:
www.brightstoryshine.com

Infographic: 6 Principles to a Trauma-informed Approach, Center for Disease Control and Prevention:
https://www.cdc.gov/cpr/infographics/6_principles_trauma_info.htm

Recovery Advocacy Project:
https://www.recoveryvoices.com/

SAMHSA's (Substance Abuse and Mental Health Services Administration) Concept of Trauma and Guidance for a Trauma-informed Approach:
https://ncsacw.samhsa.gov/userfiles/files/SAMHSA_Trauma.pdf

She Recovers Foundation:
https://sherecovers.org/

Women's Global Recovery Network:
https://www.facebook.com/groups/womensglobalrecoverynetwork

ACKNOWLEDGMENTS

What a joy to be able to write a list of gratitude as a way to complete this journey of publishing my first book. A longing fulfilled is truly a tree of life. To my tree's branches: my family (biological and otherwise) who have believed in me and walked with me in the dark. My parents: for not being surprised I wrote a book, the constant support, and for never giving up on a troubled teen. Especially my mom who has been a friend, cheerleader, and prayer warrior. To Amy and Mike Salisbury, for pointing me in the right direction. To my agent Tom Dean, runner and publishing expert extraordinaire, for taking a chance on a new author and believing in my message from the beginning. To Tess Raines, who is an editing genius, for accepting this gig with grace. The team at Morgan James Publishing, thanks for being the future. Especially, Emily Madison who is a multi-tasking legend and David Hancock for seeing possibilities. To the ladies who have inspired me: Flo Hilliard, Carolyn Boeve, Kim Ness, Rachel Kibbe, Lisa Hollman, Emily Killeen, Shelly Dutch, Nadine Machkovech, Jessica Geschke, Linda Flores, Jenna Parfitt, Kara Berry, Crystal Curry, and so many more. To my writing sisterhood at *This Grit and Grace Life* including Darlene

Brock, Ashley Johnson, Rachel Hagstrom, and Meaghan Dawson. Thank you for loving that one article I wrote that one time and then calling me. Heather Kopp, for your courage, grace, and expert writing advice. To my best boof (you know who you are) for listening to my crazy schemes and joining some of them. To a teacher who asked me this simple question once: "If you could be doing anything right now in this moment, what would it be?" To the folks at the many churches I've bopped in and out of over the years, I hope you read this. To the women who haven't survived the struggle, my words are always for you. And to my roots: my love, Matt. Thanks for believing in me and supporting me (calling me "author-mom"). You are my always. To my kids, thank you for napping well (most days) so I could write this book. I hope that when you are old enough to read this, you have met this grace I've come to know under less challenging circumstances. Regardless, it is yours.

ABOUT THE AUTHOR

Caroline Beidler, MSW is an author, recovery advocate, and Founder of *Bright Story Shine*, a storytelling platform that celebrates stories of recovery and resilience. With almost 20 years experience in leadership within social work and ministry, she provides consultation focused on creating sustainable addiction recovery support services at the local, state, and federal levels. Additionally, she is a Research Collaborator with the Lyda Hill Institute on Human Resilience at the University of Colorado, Colorado Springs and is the past Director of Wisconsin Voices for Recovery, along with a past founder and Director of ED2Recovery, a nationally recognized program that brings Recovery Coaching into hospitals and other community-based settings. Caroline was the former Chair of the Prevention Committee for the Wisconsin State Council on Alcohol and other Drug Abuse by Governor's Appointment, and has participated on many state and national coalitions and committees. She is also the founder and visionary of the *Women's Global Recovery Roundtable* event, the first ever convening of women in recovery across the globe. Caroline has a passion for young people in recovery and founded two programs for college-aged youth in recovery: Live Free – Student Wellness and Recovery (now Badger Recovery), and Connect House Sober Living Foundation, Inc., a recovery residence for college-aged women. In 2015, she won the Texas Research Society on Alcoholism, John T. and Patricia A. O'Neill Addiction Science Education Award for her research on stigma and social support for recently deployed Veterans. Her writing is featured on the *Grit and Grace Project*, *In the Rooms*, *The Fix*, the *Addiction Technology Transfer Center* and other websites. Caroline and her family live in Tennessee where she enjoys writing, hiking in the mountains, chasing around her twins Henrick and Violet, and building up her community's local recovery ministry.

Connect with her at

www.carolinebeidler.com

and

@carolinebeidler_official

and

https://www.facebook.com/carolinebeidlermsw

ENDNOTES

1   Philip Yancey, What's So Amazing About Grace (Grand Rapids: Zondervan, 2002), 68.

2   Psalms 147:3

3   Portions of this were first published with The Grit and Grace Project (2021): https://thegritandgraceproject.org/herstory/this-is-what-i-would-say-to-the-man-who-raped-me.

4   Lamentations 3:57

5   Bible Study Fellowship

6   Weber, Katherine, "Rick Warren: Why God Encourages Christians to 'Fear Not' 365 Times in the Bible," The Christian Post, 2016, https://www.christianpost.com/news/rick-warren-why-god-encourages-christians-to-fear-not-365-times-in-the-bible.html.

7   Erving, Goffman, Stigma: Notes on the management of spoiled identity (Simon and Schuster, 1963).

8   Georg Schomerus et al. "The Stigma of Alcohol Dependence Compared with Other Mental Disorders: A Review of Population Studies." Alcohol and Alcoholism, 46, no.2 (2011), 105-112, doi: 10.1093/alcalc/agq089

9   A. H. Crisp et al. (2000). "Stigmatization of People with Mental Illnesses." The British Journal of Psychiatry, 177 no. 1 (2000), 4-7, doi: 10.1192/bjp.177.1.4

10 Anne Lamott, Traveling Mercies: Some Thoughts on Faith (New York: Anchor Books, 2000),139.

11 Philip Yancey, What's So Amazing About Grace (Grand Rapids: Zondervan 2002), 68.

12 Portions of this chapter from an article first published in The Grit and Grace Project (2021): https://thegritandgraceproject. org/life-and-culture/celebrate-recovery-month-with-grace-instead-of-judgement.

13 Maria Duenas, The Time In Between (New York: Atria Books, 2012), 66.

14 Brennan Manning, All is Grace (Colorado Springs: David C. Cook, 2011), 120.

15 John 11:35

16 Jon Bloom, "Why Jesus Wept," April 29, 2011, https://www. desiringgod.org/articles/why-jesus-wept

17 Hebrews 4:15

18 https://www.weallrisetogether.org/about-us/

19 Nadine Machkovech, "The Secret to Being Enough," filmed September 2018. TED video, 18:33, https://www.youtube. com/watch?v=pbfwHMdHnv0&t=21s

20 Anne Lamott. Plan B: Further Thoughts on Faith (New York: Riverhead Books, 2005), 181-182.

21 Anne Lamott. Plan B: Further Thoughts on Faith (New York: Riverhead Books, 2005), 187.

22 Anne Lamott. Plan B: Further Thoughts on Faith (New York: Riverhead Books, 2005), 187.

23 "Understanding Addiction." Help Guide, February 8, 2022. https://www.helpguide.org/harvard/how-addiction-hijacks-the-brain.htm.

24 "Understanding Addiction." Help Guide, February 8, 2022. https://www.helpguide.org/harvard/how-addiction-hijacks-the-brain.htm.

25 Romans 7:15-20

26 A.W. Tozer, The Essential Tozer Collection: The Crucified Life (Bloomington: Bethany House Publishers, 2013), 200.

27 Retrieved from www.dictionary.com.

28 Mark 1:14-15, Romans 13:11-13, 2 Corinthians 6:1-2, Luke 12:54-56, Luke 19:44

29 Retrieved from https://www.kairoscanada.org/wp-content/uploads/2013/01/KairosBibleStudy.pdf.

30 Mark 1:15

31 John Piper, Don't Waste Your Life (Wheaton, IL: Crossway Books, 2003), 34.

32 Joanna Weaver, Having a Mary Heart in a Martha World (Colorado Springs: Waterbrook Press, 2000), 195

33 Rachel Held Evans, Searching for Sundays (Nashville, TN: Thomas Nelson, 2015).

34 Katie McCoy," God Is Not Silent: What the Bible Teaches about Sexual Assault," December 11, 2017, https://erlc.com/resource-library/articles/god-is-not-silent-what-the-bible-teaches-about-sexual-assault/

35 Katie McCoy," God Is Not Silent: What the Bible Teaches about Sexual Assault," December 11, 2017, https://erlc.com/resource-library/articles/god-is-not-silent-what-the-bible-teaches-about-sexual-assault/

36   Rev. John Henry Hanson, "Converted by Love: A Reflection on the Conversion of St. Paul," January 2, 2020, https://stjosemaria.org/converted-by-love/

37   Laura McKowen, We are the Luckiest (Novato, CA: New World Library, 2020), 74.

38   Philip Yancey, Disappointment with God, (New York, Harper-Collins,1988), 49.

39   "Dr. Paul Wilson Brand," International Leprosy Association, accessed 2021, https://leprosyhistory.org/database/person31.

40   Philip Yancey, Soul Survivor, (Colorado Springs, Waterbrook, 2003), 71.

41   Philip Yancey, "Where Is God in the Struggle of Addiction and Trauma?" interview by Caroline Beidler, Bright Story Shine, 2021. https://www.brightstoryshine.com/listen

42   Romans 8:28

43   Philip Yancey, "Where Is God in the Struggle of Addiction and Trauma?" interview by Caroline Beidler, Bright Story Shine, 2021. https://www.brightstoryshine.com/listen

44   "The Healing Forest: Recovery Community." Recovery Ways, November 7, 2016. https://www.recoveryways.com/rehab-blog/the-healing-forest-our-recovery-community/.

45   "Recovery Homes Help People in Early Recovery." SAMHSA, accessed June 5, 2022. https://www.samhsa.gov/homeless-ness-programs-resources/hpr-resources/recovery-homes-help-people.

46   Alexandre B. Laudet and Keith Humphreys. "Promoting recovery in an evolving policy context: What do we know and what do we need to know about recovery support services?" Journal of Substance Abuse Treatment, 45, no.1 (2013), 126-133, doi: 10.1016/j.jsat.2013.01.009

47 Amy A. Mericle, Jennifer Miles, and Fred Way. "Recovery Residences and Providing Safe and Supportive Housing for Individuals Overcoming Addiction." Journal of Drug Issues 45, no. 4 (2015): 368–84, doi: 10.1177/0022042615602924.

48 Amy A. Mericle, Jennifer Miles, and Fred Way. "Recovery Residences and Providing Safe and Supportive Housing for Individuals Overcoming Addiction." Journal of Drug Issues 45, no. 4 (2015): 368–84, doi: 10.1177/0022042615602924.

49 Leonard A. Jason et al. "Communal housing settings enhance substance abuse recovery." American Journal of Public Health, 96, no.10 (2006), 1727–1729, doi: 10.2105/AJPH.2005.070839

50 Douglas L. Polcin et al. "Sober living houses for alcohol and drug dependence: 18-month outcomes." Journal of Substance Abuse Treatment, 38, no. 4(2010), 356–365, doi: 10.1016/j.jsat.2010.02.003

51 Leonard A. Jason et al. "Current and Previous Residents of Self-Governed Recovery Homes: Characteristics of Long-Term Recovery," Alcoholism Treatment Quarterly, 27, no. 4(2009), 442–452, doi: 10.1080/07347320903209715

52 "Recovery and Recovery Support." SAMHSA. Accessed June 5, 2022. https://www.samhsa.gov/find-help/recovery.

53 Adam Hamilton, Incarnation (Nashville: Abingdon Press, 2020), 142.

54 Romans 7:15

55 Galatians 3:28

56 "Intro to Ruth." Biblica, May 12, 2020. https://www.biblica.com/resources/scholar-notes/niv-study-bible/intro-to-ruth/.

57 Wendy Amsellem, "The Book of Ruth: A Celebration of Female Friendship," May 28, 2014, https://www.jta.org/2014/05/28/ny/the-book-of-ruth-a-celebration-of-female-friendship

58   Ruth 1:11

59   Ruth 1:16

60   James 1:2-3

61   Carlie Terradez, 2014

62   Brennan Manning, The Wisdom of Tenderness (New York: Harper One 2004), 50

63   Johann Hari, "Everything You Think You Know About Addiction Is Wrong," filmed June 2015 in London, England, TED video, 14:33, https://www.ted.com/talks/johann_hari_ everything_you_think_you_know_about_addiction_is_ wrong?language=en

64   Robert Weiss, "The Opposite of Addiction Is Connection," Psychology Today, September 30, 2015, https://www. psychologytoday.com/us/blog/love-and-sex-in-the-digital- age/201509/the-opposite-addiction-is-connection.

65   Laura McKowen, We are the Luckiest (Novato: New World Library, 2020), 101.

66   Rosenberg, Jakob, Seymour Slive, and E.H. Ter Kuile. Dutch Art and Architecture, 1600-1800 (Harmondsworth: Penguin, 1966) 66, 80-81.

67   Henri J. M. Nouwen, The Return of the Prodigal Son: a Meditation on Fathers, Brothers, and Sons (New York: Doubleday Books, 1992) 65-66.

68   Mark 3:25

69   Only two of the four letters to the Corinthians that's alluded to in scripture have been preserved: 1 and 2 Corinthians.

70   Mark Wilson, "Treasures in Clay Jars" 2020, https://www. biblicalarchaeology.org/daily/biblical-artifacts/artifacts-and-the- bible/treasures-in-clay-jars/

71   Philip Yancey, "Is Church a Place for People Who Have Everything Together?" accessed June 6, 2022. https://churchsource.

com/blogs/ministry-resources/is-church-a-place-for-people-who-have-everything-together-philip-yancey/.

72 Portions of this chapter were first published in The Grit and Grace Project (2020): https://thegritandgraceproject.org/faith/remember-when-god-showed-up-for-you-write-that-down.

73 James Rowell, "The Israelites Who Forget, the God Who Does Not," April 6, 2020, https://generationsnorcross.com/blog/2020/04/06/the-israelites-who-forget-the-god-who-does-not.

74 Psalm 66:16

75 James 5:16

76 1 Peter 5:8

77 James 5:16

78 2 Corinthians 12:9-10

79 Bessel van der Kolk, M.D., The Body Keeps the Score: Brain, Mind, and Body in the Healing of Trauma (New York: Penguin Books, 2014), 82.

80 1 Thessalonians 5: 16-18

81 "4 Real-Life Miracle Stories That Prove the Power of Prayers and Restores Our Faith in God" October 21, 2020, https://soul.lessonslearnedinlife.com/real-life-miracle-stories-that-prove-the-power-of-prayers-and-faith-in-god-healing-back-to-life.

82 Gina Ryder, "7 Miraculous Stories about the Power of Healing Prayers," April 29, 2021. https://www.rd.com/list/prayers-for-healing/.

83 God grant me the serenity to accept the things I cannot change, the courage to change the things I can, and the wisdom to know the difference.

84 God, I offer myself to Thee—to build with me and to do with me as Thou wilt. Relieve me of the bondage of self, that I may better do Thy will. Take away my difficulties, that victory over

them may bear witness to those I would help of Thy Power, Thy Love, and Thy Way of life.

85 Luke 5:16, Matthew 26:39, Mark 1:35,

86 Philip Yancey, What's So Amazing About Grace (Grand Rapids: Zondervan, 2002), 157.

87 Eugene H. Peterson, A Long Obedience in the Same Direction: Discipleship in an Instant Society (Downers Grove: Intervarsity Press, 1980), 9.

88 Bessel van der Kolk, M.D., The Body Keeps the Score: Brain, Mind, and Body in the Healing of Trauma (New York: Penguin Books, 2014), 209.

89 Psalms 98:8-9

90 Bessel van der Kolk, M.D., The Body Keeps the Score: Brain, Mind, and Body in the Healing of Trauma (New York: Penguin Books, 2014), 206.

91 Psalm 68:5-6

92 https://www.traumainformedchurches.org/

93 https://www.tn.gov/behavioral-health/substance-abuse-services/faith-based-initiatives.html.

94 "Religious Landscape Study: Adults in Tennessee." Pew Research Center, March 31, 2022, https://www.pewresearch.org/religion/religious-landscape-study/state/tennessee/.

95 Matthew 17:20

96 Acts 9:4

97 Acts 9:11-12

98 Retrieved from www.biblegateway.com, notes on Acts 9:1-19.

99 "Break Every Chain," lyrics by Will Reagan, copyright 2009 Capitol CMG Genesis, United Pursuit Music. Used by permission.

100 Psalm 34:18

101 Isaiah 58:8

102 Henri Nouwen, Turn my Mourning into Dancing (Nashville: Thomas Nelson, 2001), 48.

103 Henri Nouwen, Following Jesus (New York: Convergent Books, 2019), 52.

104 Jeremiah 29:11

105 Brennan Manning, Abba's Child (Colorado Springs: NavPress, 2002), 30.

106 Timothy Keller, Walking with God through Pain and Suffering (New York: Penguin Books, 2013), 308.

107 Philip Yancey, What's So Amazing About Grace (Grand Rapids: Zondervan, 2002), 276-277.

A free ebook edition is available with the purchase of this book.

To claim your free ebook edition:

1. Visit MorganJamesBOGO.com
2. Sign your name CLEARLY in the space
3. Complete the form and submit a photo of the entire copyright page
4. You or your friend can download the ebook to your preferred device

Morgan James
BOGO™

A **FREE** ebook edition is available for you or a friend with the purchase of this print book.

CLEARLY SIGN YOUR NAME ABOVE

Instructions to claim your free ebook edition:
1. Visit MorganJamesBOGO.com
2. Sign your name CLEARLY in the space above
3. Complete the form and submit a photo of this entire page
4. You or your friend can download the ebook to your preferred device

Print & Digital Together Forever.

Snap a photo   Free ebook   Read anywhere

CPSIA information can be obtained
at www.ICGtesting.com
Printed in the USA
JSHW021505150523
41731JS00002B/40